General Information

Many of the products used in this pattern book can be purchased from local craft, fabric and variety stores, or from the Annie's Attic Needlecraft Catalog (see Customer Service information on page 56).

Instructions have been given for making magnets using the little motifs. The cover photos show additional ways to decorate using the motifs.

Contents

Bevy of Bugs

Bee

SKILL LEVEL

EASY

FINISHED SIZE
1¾ x 2¼ inches

MATERIALS
- Aunt Lydia's Classic Crochet size 10 crochet cotton (white: 400 yds per ball; solids: 350 yds per ball):
  10 yds each #1 white, #12 black and #422 golden yellow
- Size 7/1.65mm steel crochet hook or size needed to obtain gauge
- Tapestry needle
- Beading needle
- Darice Magnetic Canvas: #1195-03 self-adhesive 5 x 8-inch sheet
- 4mm round beads: 2 black
- Face blush
- Spray starch
- Black sewing thread
- Hot-glue gun

GAUGE
4 sc = ½ inch; 4 sc rows = ½ inch

INSTRUCTIONS
BEE BODY
Row 1: With black, ch 5, sc in 2nd ch from hook and in each ch across, turn. *(4 sc)*

Row 2: Ch 1, 2 sc in first st, sc in each st across with 2 sc in last st. Fasten off. (6 sc)

Row 3: Join golden yellow with sc in first st, sc in same st, sc in each st across with 2 sc in last st, turn. *(8 sc)*

Row 4: Ch 1, sc in each st across, turn. Fasten off.

Row 5: Join black with sc in first st, sc in each st across, turn.

Row 6: Ch 1, sc in each st across, turn. Fasten off.

Rows 7 & 8: With golden yellow, rep rows 5 and 6.

Rows 9 & 10: Rep rows 5 and 6.

Row 11: Join golden yellow with sc in first st, sc in each st across, turn.

Rows 12 & 13: Ch 1, sc in each st across, turn.

Rows 14 & 15: Ch 1, **sc dec** *(see Stitch Guide)* in first 2 sts, sc in each st across to last 2 sts, sc dec in last 2 sts, turn. Fasten off at end of last row. *(4 sc at end of last row)*

WINGS
Rnd 1: With white, ch 7, 3 hdc in 2nd ch from hook, sc in each of next 4 chs, (3 hdc, ch 1, 3 hdc) in last ch, working on opposite side of ch, sc in each of next 4 chs, 3 hdc in last ch, ch 1, join with sl st in top of beg hdc. *(12 hdc, 8 sc, 2 ch sps)*

Rnd 2: Ch 2 *(counts as first hdc)* hdc in same st, 2 hdc in each of next 2 sts, sc in each of next 4 sts, 2 hdc in each of next 3 sts, 2 hdc in next ch sp, 2 hdc in each of next 3 sts, sc in each of next 4 sts, 2 hdc in each of next 3 sts, 2 hdc in next ch sp, join with sl st in 2nd ch of beg ch-2. Fasten off.

ASSEMBLY

1. Spray Bee and Wings lightly with starch, shape; let dry.

2. With black, using **backstitch** *(see Fig. 1)*, embroider mouth over rnds 12–14 as shown in photo.

3. Sew eyes side by side to top of head centered above mouth for eyes.

4. Glue Wings to back of Body.

5. Brush cheeks of Bee with blush.

6. Using Bee as pattern, cut piece magnetic canvas 1/8 inch smaller around outer edge. Attach to back of Bee. ■

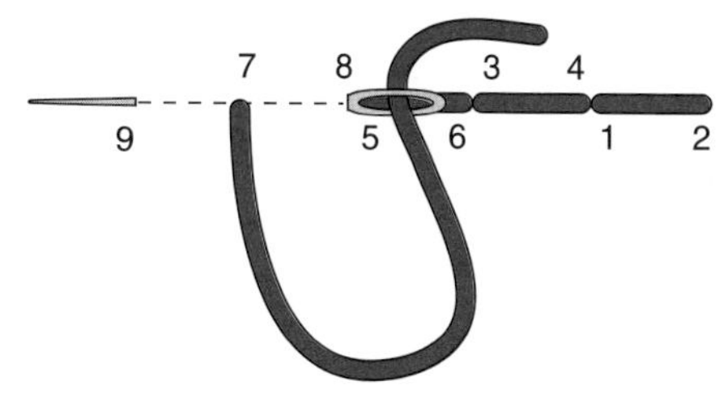

Fig. 1
Backstitch

Butterfly

SKILL LEVEL

FINISHED SIZE
1¾ x 2⅜ inches

MATERIALS

- Aunt Lydia's Classic Crochet size 10 crochet cotton (solids: 350 yds per ball; multis: 300 yds per ball):
  - 15 yds #250 Mexicana
  - 5 yds #12 black
- Sizes 10/1.15mm and 7/1.65mm steel crochet hooks or size needed to obtain gauge
- Tapestry needle
- Darice Magnetic Canvas: #1195-03 self-adhesive 5 x 8-inch sheet
- 24-gauge wire: 1¼ inches black
- Spray starch
- Hot-glue gun

GAUGE
Size 7 hook: 4 sc = ½ inch

INSTRUCTIONS

LOWER WING

MAKE 2.

Row 1: With size 7 hook and Mexicana, ch 2, (sc, hdc, dc, 2 tr, ch 1, 2 tr, dc, hdc, sc) in 2nd ch from hook, turn. *(10 sts)*

Row 2: Ch 1, 2 sc in first st, 2 hdc in next st, 2 dc in next st, 2 tr in each of next 2 sts, 2 tr in next ch sp, 2 tr in each of next 2 sts, 2 dc in next st, 2 hdc in next st, 2 sc in next st, ch 1, sc in side of last sc, sc in sp between last and first sc, sc in side of beg sc. Fasten off. *(25 sts)*

UPPER WING
MAKE 2.

Row 1: With size 7 hook and Mexicana, ch 2, (sc, hdc, dc, 2 tr, ch 1, 2 tr, dc, hdc, sc) in 2nd ch from hook, turn. *(10 sts)*

Row 2: Ch 1, 2 sc in first st, 2 hdc in next st, 2 dc in next st, 2 tr in each of next 2 sts, (tr, ch 3, sl st in 3rd ch from hook, tr) in next ch sp, 2 tr in each of next 2 sts, 2 dc in next st, 2 hdc in next st, 2 sc in next st, ch 1, sc in side of last sc, sc in sp between last and first sc, sc in side of beg sc. Fasten off. *(25 sts)*

BODY

With size 10 hook and black, ch 15, sc in 2nd ch from hook and in each ch across with 2 sc in last ch, working on opposite side of ch, sc in each ch across. Fasten off.

ASSEMBLY

1. Tack last 3 sts of Lower Wings tog. Rep on Upper Wings.

2. Overlapping Upper Wings slightly over Lower Wings, sew Body to center top of Wings through all thicknesses *(see photo)*.

3. Spray Butterfly lightly with starch, shape; let dry.

4. Bend wire into "V" shape. Curl each end of wire and glue bottom point of wire to back side on end of Body to form antennae on each side of head.

5. Using Butterfly as pattern, cut piece magnetic canvas 1⁄8 inch smaller around outer edge. Attach to back of Butterfly. ■

Dragonfly

SKILL LEVEL

EASY

FINISHED SIZE

1¾ x 2 inches

MATERIALS

- Aunt Lydia's Classic Crochet size 10 crochet cotton (350 yds per ball):
  5 yds each #479 bridal blue and #458 purple
- Size 7/1.65mm steel crochet hook or size needed to obtain gauge
- Tapestry needle
- Beading needle
- Darice Magnetic Canvas:
  #1195-03 self-adhesive 5 x 8-inch sheet
- 2 black seed beads
- Spray starch
- Black sewing thread

GAUGE

4 hdc = 7⁄16 inch; 3 hdc rows = ½ inch

PATTERN NOTE

Chain-2 at beginning of row counts as first half double crochet unless otherwise stated.

INSTRUCTIONS
WING
MAKE 2.

Row 1: With purple, ch 2, 2 hdc in 2nd ch from hook, turn. *(2 hdc)*

Row 2: **Ch 2** *(see Pattern Note)*, hdc in same st, 2 hdc in last st, turn. *(4 hdc)*

Rows 3–11: Ch 2, hdc in each st across, turn.

Row 12: Ch 2, **hdc dec** *(see Stitch Guide)* in last 2 sts. Fasten off.

BODY

With bridal blue, ch 15, sl st in 2nd ch from hook and in each of next 12 chs, 7 hdc in last ch, working on opposite side of ch, hdc in next 13 chs, join with sl st in beg sl st. Fasten off.

ASSEMBLY

1. Spray Wings and Body lightly with starch, shape; let dry.

2. With Wings held tog, wrap strand purple tightly around middle of Wings several times and secure ends.

3. Pull ends of Wings to form upper and lower Wings *(see photo)*. Sew Wings centered to top of Body below 7-hdc group.

4. Sew beads to top end of Body over 7-hdc group for eyes.

5. Using Dragonfly as pattern, cut piece magnetic canvas ⅛ inch smaller around outer edge. Attach to back of Dragonfly. ■

Ladybug

SKILL LEVEL

EASY

FINISHED SIZE

1¾ x 1⅜ inches

MATERIALS

- Aunt Lydia's Classic Crochet size 10 crochet cotton (350 yds per ball):
  10 yds each #494 victory red and #210 antique white
- Size 7/1.65mm steel crochet hook or size needed to obtain gauge
- Tapestry needle
- Beading needle
- Darice Magnetic Canvas:
  #1195-03 self-adhesive 5 x 8-inch sheet
- 4mm round beads: 2 black
- 6mm acrylic cabochon: 6 black
- Face blush
- 24-gauge wire: 1¼ inches black
- Spray starch
- Black sewing thread
- Hot-glue gun

GAUGE

4 hdc = ½ inch; 3 hdc rows = ½ inch

PATTERN NOTE

Chain-2 at beginning of row counts as first half double crochet unless otherwise stated.

INSTRUCTIONS

BODY

Row 1: With victory red, ch 15, hdc in 2nd ch from hook and in each ch across, turn. *(14 hdc)*

Rows 2–5: **Ch 2** *(see Pattern Note)*, hdc in each st across, turn.

Rows 6–8: Ch 2, **hdc dec** *(see Stitch Guide)* in next 2 sts, hdc in each st across to last 2 sts, hdc dec in last 2 sts, turn. Fasten off at end of last row. *(8 hdc at end of last row)*

HEAD

Row 1: With antique white, ch 9, sc in 2nd ch from hook and in each ch across, turn. *(8 sc)*

Rows 2–5: Ch 1, sc in each st across, turn.

Rows 6 & 7: Ch 1, **sc dec** *(see Stitch Guide)* in first 2 sts, sc in each st across to last 2 sts, sc dec in last 2 sts, turn. *(4 sc at end of last row)*

Row 8: Ch 1, sc dec in first 2 sts, sc dec in last 2 sts. Fasten off.

ASSEMBLY

1. Spray Body and Head lightly with starch, shape; let dry.

2. With victory red, using **straight stitch** *(see Fig. 1)*, embroider mouth over rnds 3–6 of Head as shown in photo.

Fig. 1
Straight Stitch

3. Sew 4mm beads side-by-side to Head centered above mouth for eyes.

4. Bend wire into "V" shape. Curl each end of wire and glue bottom point of wire to top back side of Head to form antennae on each side of Head.

5. Brush cheeks of Ladybug with blush.

6. With bottom edges even, glue Head centered to top of Body.

7. Glue cabochons evenly sp around Body above Head *(see photo)*.

8. Using Ladybug as pattern, cut piece magnetic canvas ⅛ inch smaller around outer edge. Attach to back of Ladybug. ■

Snail

SKILL LEVEL

EASY

FINISHED SIZE

1½ x 1⅝ inches

MATERIALS

- Aunt Lydia's Classic Crochet size 10 crochet cotton (350 yds per ball):
  5 yds each #397 wasabi, #484 myrtle green and #422 golden yellow
- Size 7/1.65mm steel crochet hook or size needed to obtain gauge
- Beading needle
- Darice Magnetic Canvas:
  #1195-03 self-adhesive 5 x 8-inch sheet
- 4mm round bead: 1 black
- 24-gauge wire: 1¼ inches black
- Spray starch
- Black sewing thread
- Stitch marker
- Hot-glue gun

GAUGE

5 sc = ½ inch; 3 sc rows = ½ inch

PATTERN NOTES

Work in **back loops** *(see Stitch Guide)* unless otherwise stated.

Do not join or turn unless otherwise stated. Mark first stitch of each round.

INSTRUCTIONS

SHELL

Rnd 1: With myrtle green, ch 2, 10 sc in 2nd ch from hook, **change color** *(see Stitch Guide)* to wasabi in last st. *(10 sc)*

Rnd 2: 2 sc in each st around, changing to myrtle green in last st. *(20 sc)*

Rnd 3: 2 sc in first st, sc in next st, [2 sc in next st, sc in next st] around, changing to wasabi in last st. *(30 sc)*

Rnd 4: 2 sc in first st, sc in each of next 2 sts, [2 sc in next st, sc in each of next 2 sts] around, changing to myrtle green in last st. *(40 sc)*

Rnd 5: 2 sc in first st, sc in each of next 3 sts, [2 sc in next st, sc in each of next 3 sts] around, join with sl st in beg sc. Fasten off. *(50 sc)*

BODY

Join golden yellow with sl st in both lps of 15th st of last row on Shell, ch 2 *(counts as first hdc)*, for **head**, 12 hdc in same st, working in back lps, hdc in each of next 11 sts, sc in next st, sl st in next st. Fasten off.

TAIL

Sk next 8 sts on last row of Shell, join golden yellow with sl st in next st, (ch 1, hdc, sl st) in same st. Fasten off.

ASSEMBLY

1. Spray Snail lightly with starch, shape; let dry.

2. Sew bead to head for eye.

3. Bend wire into "V" shape. Curl each end of wire and glue bottom point of wire to back side of head to form antennae on each side of head.

4. Using Snail as pattern, cut piece magnetic canvas 1/8 inch smaller around outer edge. Attach to back of Snail. ■

By the Sea

Anchor

SKILL LEVEL

EASY

FINISHED SIZE

1¼ x 2 inches

MATERIALS

- Aunt Lydia's Classic Crochet size 10 crochet cotton (350 yds per ball):
  10 yds #449 forest green
- Size 10/1.15mm steel crochet hook or size needed to obtain gauge
- Darice Magnetic Canvas:
  #1195-03 self-adhesive 5 x 8-inch sheet
- Spray starch

GAUGE

5 sc = ½ inch; 5 sc rows = ½ inch

INSTRUCTIONS

ANCHOR

Row 1: Ch 5, 2 sc in 2nd ch from hook, sc in each of next 2 chs, 2 sc in last ch, turn. *(6 sc)*

Rows 2–4: Ch 1, 2 sc in first st, sc in each st across with 2 sc in last st, turn. *(12 sc at end of last row)*

FIRST POINT

Row 1: Ch 1, sc in each of first 2 sts, leaving rem sts unworked, turn. *(2 sc)*

Row 2: Ch 3, sl st in 2nd ch from hook, sc in next ch, (hdc, dc) in next st, ch 1, (dc, hdc) in last st, ch 3, sl st in 2nd ch from hook, sl st in same st as last hdc. Fasten off.

2ND POINT

Row 1: Sk next 8 sts on last row of Anchor, join with sc in next st, sc in last st, turn. *(2 sc)*

Row 2: Ch 3, sl st in 2nd ch from hook, sc in next ch, (hdc, dc) in next st, ch 1, (dc, hdc) in last st, ch 3, sl st in 2nd ch from hook, sl st in same st as last hdc. Fasten off.

CENTER

Row 1: Working in center 2 unworked sts on row 4 of Anchor, join with sc in first st, sc in next st, turn. *(2 sc)*

Rows 2–7: Ch 1, sc in each st across, turn. Fasten off.

Row 8: Ch 3, join with sc in first st on row 7, sc in next st, ch 4, turn.

Row 9: Sc in 2nd ch from hook and in each of next 2 chs, sc in each of next 2 sts, sc in each of next 3 chs, turn. *(8 sc)*

Row 10: Ch 1, sc in each st across. Fasten off.

HANGING LOOP

Row 1: Join with sl st in 3rd st of last row on Center, ch 6, sk next 2 sts, sl st in next st, turn. *(2 sl sts, 1 ch sp)*

Row 2: Ch 1, sl st in each of next 5 chs, sl st in same st as first st on row 1. Fasten off.

ASSEMBLY

1. Spray Anchor lightly with starch, shape; let dry.

2. Using Anchor as pattern, cut piece magnetic canvas 1/8 inch smaller around outer edge. Attach to back of Anchor. ■

Dolphin

SKILL LEVEL

EASY

FINISHED SIZE

1¾ x 3 inches

MATERIALS

- Aunt Lydia's Classic Crochet size 10 crochet cotton (350 yds per ball):
  10 yds each #1056 chambray and #479 bridal blue
- Size 7/1.65mm steel crochet hook or size needed to obtain gauge
- Beading needle
- Darice Magnetic Canvas:
  #1195-03 self-adhesive 5 x 8-inch sheet
- 4mm round bead: 1 black
- Spray starch
- Black sewing thread

GAUGE

4 sc = ½ inch; 4 sc rows = ½ inch

INSTRUCTIONS

LOWER BODY

Row 1: With bridal blue, ch 2, 3 sc in 2nd ch from hook, turn. *(3 sc)*

Rows 2 & 3: Ch 1, sc in each st across, turn.

Row 4: Ch 1, 2 sc in first st, sc in next st, 2 sc in last st, turn. *(5 sc)*

Rows 5–15: Ch 1, sc in each st across, turn.

Row 16: Ch 1, **sc dec** *(see Stitch Guide)* in first 2 sts, sc in next st, sc dec in last 2 sts, turn. *(3 sc)*

Row 17: Ch 1, sc in first st, sc dec in last 2 sts, turn. *(2 sc)*

Row 18: Ch 1, sc dec in next 2 sts, turn. Fasten off.

UPPER BODY

Row 1: Join chambray with sl st in first st of last row on Lower Body, ch 3, hdc in 2nd ch from hook, hdc in next ch, hdc in same st as joining, working in ends of rows, evenly sp 8 sc across next 7 rows, 3 sc in next row, evenly sp 8 sc across rem rows, turn. *(22 sts)*

Row 2: Ch 2 *(counts as first hdc)*, hdc in each of next 16 sts, **hdc dec** *(see Stitch Guide)* in next 2 sts, leaving rem sts unworked, turn. *(18 hdc)*

Row 3: Ch 2, hdc dec in next 2 sts, hdc in each of next 5 sts, ch 7, sl st in 2nd ch from hook, [sc dec in next 2 chs] twice, hdc in next ch, hdc in side of last hdc made, hdc in each of next 4 sts on last row, sc in next st, sl st in next st, leaving rem sts unworked. Fasten off.

TAIL

Row 1: Join chambray with sc in end of first st on row 2 of Upper Body, sc in end of next row, sc in next ch on opposite side of starting ch on Lower Body, turn. *(3 sc)*

Row 2: Ch 4 *(counts as first tr)*, (2 tr, 2 dc) in same st, sl st in next st, (2 dc, 3 tr) in last st. Fasten off.

ASSEMBLY

1. Spray Dolphin lightly with starch, shape; let dry.

2. For **eye**, sew bead to row 1 of Upper Body *(see photo)*.

3. Using Dolphin as pattern, cut piece magnetic canvas 1/8 inch smaller around outer edge. Attach to back of Dolphin. ■

Lighthouse

SKILL LEVEL

EASY

FINISHED SIZE

1¼ x 3⅜ inches

MATERIALS

- Aunt Lydia's Classic Crochet size 10 crochet cotton (white: 400 yds per ball; solids: 350 yds per ball):
  - 10 yds #12 black
  - 5 yds each #1 white and #421 goldenrod
- Size 7/1.65mm steel crochet hook or size needed to obtain gauge
- Darice Magnetic Canvas: #1195-03 self-adhesive 5 x 8-inch sheet
- Spray starch

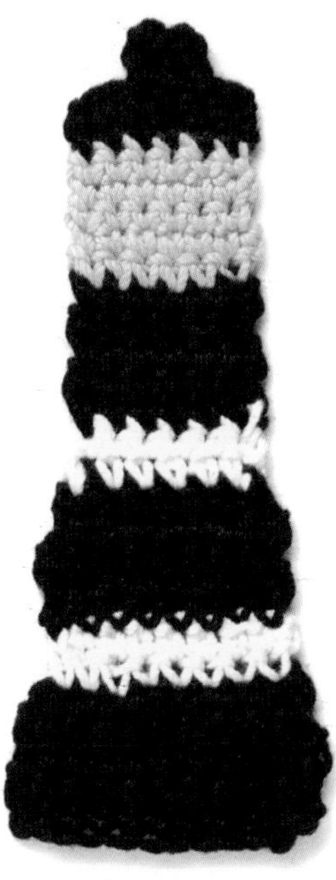

GAUGE

4 sc = ½ inch; 4 sc rows = ½ inch

INSTRUCTIONS

LIGHTHOUSE

Row 1: With black, ch 11, sc in 2nd ch from hook and in each ch across, turn. *(10 sc)*

Rows 2–4: Ch 1, sc in each st across, turn.

Row 5: Ch 1, **sc dec** *(see Stitch Guide)* in first 2 sts, sc in each st across to last 2 sts, sc dec in last 2 sts, turn. Fasten off. *(8 sc)*

Row 6: Join white with sc in first st, sc in each st across, turn.

Row 7: Ch 1, sc in each st across, turn. Fasten off.

Row 8: Join black with sc in first st, sc in each st across, turn.

Rows 9–11: Ch 1, sc in each st across, turn.

Row 12: Rep row 5. *(6 sc)*

Row 13: Join white with sc in first st, sc in each st across, turn.

Row 14: Ch 1, sc in each st across, turn. Fasten off.

Row 15: Join black with sc in first st, sc in each st across, turn.

Rows 16–19: Ch 1, sc in each st across, turn. Fasten off at end of last row.

Row 20: Join goldenrod with sc in first st, sc in each st across, turn.

Rows 21–24: Ch 1, sc in each st across, turn. Fasten off at end of last row.

Row 25: Join black with sc in first st, sc in each st across, turn.

Row 26: Ch 1, sc in each st across, turn.

Row 27: Sl st in next st, ch 3 *(counts as first dc)*, dc in each of next 2 sts, leaving rem sts unworked. Fasten off.

ASSEMBLY

1. Spray Lighthouse lightly with starch, shape; let dry.

2. Using Lighthouse as pattern, cut piece magnetic canvas 1/8 inch smaller around outer edge. Attach to back of Lighthouse. ■

Sailboat

SKILL LEVEL

EASY

FINISHED SIZE

2 x 2 inches

MATERIALS

- Aunt Lydia's Classic Crochet size 10 crochet cotton (white: 400 yds per ball; solids: 350 yds per ball; multis: 300 yds per ball):
  - 5 yds each #431 pumpkin, #250 Mexicana and white #1
- Size 7/1.65mm steel crochet hook or size needed to obtain gauge
- Darice Magnetic Canvas:
  - #1195-03 self-adhesive 5 x 8-inch sheet
- Spray starch
- Hot-glue gun

GAUGE

4 sc = 1/2 inch; 4 sc rows = 1/2 inch

PATTERN NOTE

Chain-2 at beginning of row counts as first half double crochet unless otherwise stated.

INSTRUCTIONS

BOAT

Row 1: With pumpkin, ch 16, sc in 2nd ch from hook and in each of next 3 chs, hdc in each of last 11 chs, turn. *(11 hdc, 4 sc)*

Row 2: **Ch 2** *(see Pattern Note)*, **hdc dec** *(see Stitch Guide)* in next 2 sts, hdc in each of next 7 sts, hdc dec in next 2 sts, leaving rem sts unworked, turn. *(10 hdc)*

Row 3: Ch 2, hdc dec in next 2 sts, hdc in each of next 5 sts, hdc dec in last 2 sts. Fasten off.

MAST

With white, ch 14, sc in 2nd ch from hook and in each ch across. Fasten off. *(13 sc)*

LARGE SAIL

Row 1: Join Mexicana with sc in 2nd st of Mast, sc in each of next 8 sts, leaving rem sts unworked, turn. *(9 sc)*

Row 2: Ch 1, sc in each st across to last 2 sts, **sc dec** *(see Stitch Guide)* in last 2 sts, turn. *(8 sc)*

Row 3: Ch 1, sk first st, sc in each st across, turn. *(7 sc)*

Rows 4–7: [Rep rows 2 and 3 alternately] twice. *(3 sc at end of last row)*

Row 8: Ch 1, sc in first st, sc dec in last 2 sts, turn. *(2 sc)*

Row 9: Ch 1, sc dec in next 2 sts. Fasten off.

SMALL SAIL

Row 1: Working on opposite side of starting ch on Mast, sk first 3 chs, join Mexicana with sc in next ch, sc in each of next 6 chs, leaving rem chs unworked, turn. *(7 chs)*

Row 2: Ch 1, sk first st, sc in each st across, turn. *(6 sc)*

Row 3: Ch 1, sc in each st across to last 2 sts, sc dec in last 2 sts, turn. *(5 sc)*

Rows 4 & 5: Rep rows 2 and 3. *(3 sc at end of last row)*

Row 6: Ch 1, sk first st, sc in each of last 2 sts, turn. *(2 sc)*

Row 7: Ch 1, sc dec in next 2 sts. Fasten off.

FLAG

Sk next ch on starting ch of Mast, join pumpkin with sl st in next ch, ch 3, sl st 2nd ch from hook, sl st in next ch, sl st in next ch on Mast. Fasten off.

ASSEMBLY

1. Spray Boat and Sails lightly with starch, shape; let dry.

2. Glue end of Mast to last row of Boat on WS *(see photo)*.

3. Using Sailboat as pattern, cut piece magnetic canvas 1⁄8 inch smaller around outer edge. Attach to back of Sailboat. ■

Starfish

SKILL LEVEL

EASY

FINISHED SIZE

2¼ x 2¼ inches

MATERIALS

- Aunt Lydia's Classic Crochet size 10 crochet cotton (350 yds per ball):
  10 yds #21 linen
- Size 10/1.15mm steel crochet hook or size needed to obtain gauge
- Darice Magnetic Canvas:
  #1195-03 self-adhesive 5 x 8-inch sheet
- Spray starch

GAUGE

3 sc = ¼ inch; 3 sc rows = ¼ inch

PATTERN NOTE

Join with slip stitch as indicated unless otherwise stated.

INSTRUCTIONS

STARFISH

Rnd 1: Ch 2, 5 sc in 2nd ch from hook, **join** *(see Pattern Note)* in beg sc. *(5 sc)*

Rnd 2: Ch 1, 2 sc in each st around, join in beg sc. *(10 sc)*

Rnd 3: Ch 1, 2 sc in first st, sc in next st, [2 sc in next st, sc in next st] around, join in beg sc. *(15 sc)*

Rnd 4: Ch 1, 2 sc in first st, sc in each of next 2 sts, [2 sc in next st, sc in each of next 2 sts] around, join in beg sc. *(20 sc)*

Rnd 5: Ch 1, for **points**, (sc, ch 6, sc in 2nd ch from hook, sc in next ch, hdc in each of next 3 chs, hdc) in first st, sc in each of next 3 sts, *(sc, ch 6, sc in 2nd ch from hook, sc in next ch, hdc in each of next 3 chs, hdc) in next st, sc in each of next 3 sts, rep from * around, join in beg sc. *(5 points)*

Rnd 6: Ch 1, sc in first st, *working on opposite side of next ch-6, sc in each of next 3 chs, 2 sc in next ch, 2 sc in next st on point**, sc in each of next 9 sts, rep from * around, ending last rep **, sc in each of last 8 sts, join in beg sc. *(80 sc)*

Rnd 7: *Sc in each of next 4 sts, 2 sc in each of next 2 sts, sc in each of next 6 sts**, sl st in each of next 4 sts, rep from * around, ending last rep at **, sl st in each of last 3 sts, join with sl st in joining sl st of last rnd. Fasten off.

ASSEMBLY

1. Spray Starfish lightly with starch, shape; let dry.

2. Using Starfish as pattern, cut piece magnetic canvas ⅛ inch smaller around outer edge. Attach to back of Starfish. ■

Shapes & Signs

Diamond in a Square

SKILL LEVEL

EASY

FINISHED SIZE
1⅜ inches square

MATERIALS
- Kreinik Metallics #16 medium braid (11 yds/10m per spool)
  1 spool each #008HL green hi lustre and #001HL silver hi lustre
- Size 7/1.65mm steel crochet hook or size needed to obtain gauge
- Darice Magnetic Canvas: #1195-03 self-adhesive 5 x 8-inch sheet

GAUGE
4 sc = ½ inch; 4 sc rows = ½ inch

INSTRUCTIONS
DIAMOND
Row 1: With green, ch 6, sc in 2nd ch from hook and in each ch across, turn. *(5 sc)*

Rows 2–4: Ch 1, sc in each st across, turn. Fasten off at end of last row.

POINT
Row 1: Working on 1 side of Diamond, join silver with sc in corner before 1 side, evenly sp 4 sc across to next corner, turn. *(5 sc)*

Row 2: Ch 1, sk first st, sc in each of next 2 sts, **sc dec** *(see Stitch Guide)* in last 2 sts, turn. *(3 sc)*

Row 3: Ch 1, sc in first st, sc dec in last 2 sts, turn. *(2 sc)*

Row 4: Ch 1, sc dec in next 2 sts. Fasten off.

Rep Point on each rem side of Diamond.

EDGING
Join green with sc in top of any Point, ch 1, sc in same st, evenly sp 9 sc across to tip of next Point, *(sc, ch 1, sc) in tip of next Point, evenly sp 9 sc across to tip of next Point, rep from * around, join in beg sc. Fasten off.

ASSEMBLY
Using Diamond in a Square as pattern, cut piece magnetic canvas ⅛ inch smaller around outer edge. Attach to back of Diamond in a Square. ■

Copper Coin

SKILL LEVEL

EASY

FINISHED SIZE
1¾ inches in diameter

MATERIALS
- Kreinik Metallics #16 medium braid (11 yds/10m per spool)
  1 spool #021HL copper hi lustre
- Size 7/1.65mm steel crochet hook or size needed to obtain gauge
- Darice Magnetic Canvas:
  #1195-03 self-adhesive 5 x 8-inch sheet

GAUGE
5 sc = ½ inch; 3 sc rows = ½ inch

PATTERN NOTE
Join with slip stitch as indicated unless otherwise stated.

INSTRUCTIONS
COIN SIDE
MAKE 2.
Rnd 1: Ch 2, 5 sc in 2nd ch from hook, **join** *(see Pattern Note)* in beg sc. *(5 sc)*

Rnd 2: Ch 1, 2 sc in each st around, join in beg sc. *(10 sc)*

Rnd 3: Ch 1, 2 sc in first st, sc in next st, [2 sc in next st, sc in next st] around, join in beg sc. *(15 sc)*

Rnd 4: Ch 1, 2 sc in first st, sc in each of next 2 sts, [2 sc in next st, sc in each of next 2 sts] around, join in beg sc. *(20 sc)*

Rnd 5: Ch 1, 2 sc in first st, sc in each of next 3 sts, [2 sc in next st, sc in each of next 3 sts] around, join in beg sc. *(25 sc)*

Rnd 6: Ch 1, 2 sc in first st, sc in each of next 4 sts, [2 sc in next st, sc in each of next 4 sts] around, join in beg sc. Fasten off. *(30 sc)*

ASSEMBLY
1. Holding Coin Sides WS tog, matching sts, working through both thicknesses, sl st tog.

2. Using Coin as pattern, cut piece magnetic canvas ⅛ inch smaller around outer edge. Attach to back of Coin. ■

Heart Photo Frame

SKILL LEVEL

EASY

FINISHED SIZE

2½ x 2½ inches

MATERIALS

- Kreinik Metallics #16 medium braid (11 yds/10m per spool)
  2 spools #024HL fuchsia hi lustre
- Size 7/1.65mm steel crochet hook or size needed to obtain gauge
- Darice Magnetic Canvas:
  #1195-03 self-adhesive 5 x 8-inch sheet

GAUGE

4 sc = ½ inch; 4 sc rows = ½ inch

INSTRUCTIONS

HEART FRAME BACK

Row 1: Ch 2, 3 sc in 2nd ch from hook. *(3 sc)*

Row 2: Ch 1, 2 sc in first st, sc in next st, 2 sc in last st, turn. *(5 sc)*

Row 3: Ch 1, sc in each st across, turn.

Row 4: Ch 1, 2 sc in first st, sc in each st across with 2 sc in last st, turn. *(7 sc)*

Row 5: Ch 1, sc in each st across, turn.

Rows 6–13: [Rep rows 4 and 5 alternately] 4 times. *(15 sc at end of last row)*

FIRST HEART LOBE

Row 1: Ch 1, **sc dec** *(see Stitch Guide)* in first 2 sts, sc in each of next 4 sts, sc dec in next 2 sts, leaving rem sts unworked, turn. *(6 sc)*

Row 2: Ch 1, sc dec in first 2 sts, sc in each of next 2 sts, sc dec in next 2 sts, turn. *(4 sc)*

Row 3: Ch 1, sc dec in first 2 sts, sc dec in last 2 sts. Fasten off.

2ND HEART LOBE

Row 1: Join with sl st in same st as last worked st on row 13 of Heart Frame Back, ch 1, sc dec in same st and next st, sc in each of next 4 sts, sc dec in last 2 sts, turn. *(6 sc)*

Rows 2 & 3: Rep rows 2 and 3 of First Heart Lobe.

HEART FRAME FRONT

Row 1: Ch 2, 3 sc in 2nd ch from hook. *(3 sc)*

Row 2: Ch 1, 2 sc in first st, sc in next st, 2 sc in last st, turn. *(5 sc)*

Row 3: Ch 1, sc in each st across, turn.

Row 4: Ch 1, 2 sc in first st, sc in each st across with 2 sc in last st, turn. *(7 sc)*

Row 5: Ch 1, sc in each st across, turn.

Row 6: Rep row 4. *(9 sc)*

FIRST SIDE

Row 1: Ch 1, 2 sc in first st, sc in next st, leaving rem sts unworked, turn. *(3 sc)*

Row 2: Ch 1, sc in each st across, turn.

Row 3: Ch 1, 2 sc in first st, sc in each of next 2 sts, turn. *(4 sc)*

Row 4: Ch 1, sc in each st across, turn.

Row 5: Ch 1, 2 sc in first st, sc in each st across, turn. *(5 sc)*

Row 6: Ch 1, sc in each st across. Fasten off.

2ND SIDE

Row 1: Sk next 5 unworked sts of row 6 on Heart Frame Front, join with sc in next st, 2 sc in last st, turn. *(3 sc)*

Row 2: Ch 1, sc in each st across, turn.

Row 3: Ch 1, sc in each st across with 2 sc in last st, turn. *(4 sc)*

Rows 4 & 5: Rep rows 2 and 3. *(5 sc)*

Row 6: Ch 1, sc in each st across, turn.

Row 7: Ch 1, sc in each st across, ch 5, sc in each st across First Side, turn. *(10 sc, 5 chs)*

FIRST HEART LOBE

Row 1: Ch 1, sc dec in first 2 sts, sc in each of next 4 sts or chs, sc dec in next 2 chs, leaving rem sts unworked, turn. *(6 sc)*

Row 2: Ch 1, sc dec in first 2 sts, sc in each of next 2 sts, sc dec in next 2 sts, turn. *(4 sc)*

Row 3: Ch 1, sc dec in first 2 sts, sc dec in last 2 sts. Fasten off.

2ND HEART LOBE

Row 1: Join with sl st in same ch as last worked st on row 7 of Heart Frame 2nd Side, ch 1, sc dec in same ch and next ch, sc in each of next 4 sts or chs, sc dec in last 2 sts, turn. *(6 sc)*

Rows 2 & 3: Rep rows 2 and 3 of First Heart Lobe.

EDGING

Hold Front and Back Heart Frames tog, matching sts, working through both thicknesses, join with sc in any st, ch 3, (sc, ch 3) evenly sp around entire outer edge, spacing sc approximately 1/4 inch apart, join with sl st in beg sc, inserting picture into Frame before closing. Fasten off.

ASSEMBLY

Using Heart Frame as pattern, cut piece magnetic canvas 1/8 inch smaller around outer edge. Attach to back of Frame. ■

Red Arrow

SKILL LEVEL

FINISHED SIZE

1¼ x 2½ inches in diameter

MATERIALS

- Kreinik Metallics #16 medium braid (11 yds/10m per spool)
  1 spool #003HL red hi lustre
- Size 7/1.65mm steel crochet hook or size needed to obtain gauge
- Darice Magnetic Canvas:
  #1195-03 self-adhesive 5 x 8-inch sheet

GAUGE

4 sc = ½ inch; 4 sc rows = ½ inch

INSTRUCTIONS

ARROW

Row 1: Ch 2, 3 sc in 2nd ch from hook, turn. *(3 sc)*

Row 2: Ch 1, 2 sc in first st, sc in next st, 2 sc in last st, turn. *(5 sc)*

Rows 3 & 4: Ch 1, 2 sc in first st, sc in each st across with 2 sc in last st, turn. *(9 sc at end of last row)*

Row 5: Ch 1, 2 sc in first st, sc in each st across with 2 sc in last st, **do not turn**. Fasten off. *(11 sc)*

Row 6: Sk first 3 sts, join with sc in next st, sc in each of next 4 sts, leaving last 3 sts unworked, turn. *(5 sc)*

Rows 7–17: Ch 1, sc in each st across, turn. Fasten off at end of last row.

ASSEMBLY

Using Arrow as pattern, cut piece magnetic canvas 1/8 inch smaller around outer edge. Attach to back of Arrow. ■

Star

SKILL LEVEL

EASY

FINISHED SIZE

2 x 2 inches

MATERIALS

- Kreinik Metallics #16 medium braid (11 yds/10m per spool)
  1 spool #051HL sapphire hi lustre
- Size 7/1.65mm steel crochet hook or size needed to obtain gauge
- Darice Magnetic Canvas:
  #1195-03 self-adhesive 5 x 8-inch sheet

GAUGE

4 sc = 1/2 inch; 4 sc rows = 1/2 inch

PATTERN NOTE

Join with slip stitch as indicated unless otherwise stated.

INSTRUCTIONS

STAR

Rnd 1: Ch 2, 5 sc in 2nd ch from hook, **join** *(see Pattern Note)* in beg sc. *(5 sc)*

Rnd 2: Ch 1, 2 sc in each st around, join in beg sc. *(10 sc)*

Rnd 3: Ch 1, 2 sc in first st, sc in next st, [2 sc in next st, sc in next st] around join in beg sc. *(15 sc)*

Rnd 4: Ch 1, 2 sc in first st, sc in each of next 2 sts, [2 sc in next st, sc in each of next 2 sts] around, join in beg sc. Fasten off. *(20 sc)*

FIRST POINT

Row 1: Ch 1, sc in each of first 4 sts, leaving rem sts unworked, turn. *(4 sc)*

Row 2: Ch 1, sk first st, sc in next st, **sc dec** *(see Stitch Guide)* in last 2 sts, turn. *(2 sc)*

Row 3: Ch 1, sc in each st across, turn.

Row 4: Ch 1, sk first st, sc in next st. Fasten off.

NEXT POINT

Row 1: Join with sc in next unworked st on rnd 4 of Star, sc in each of next 3 sts, leaving rem sts unworked, turn. *(4 sc)*

Rows 2–4: Rep rows 2–4 of First Point.

Rep Next Point 3 more times for a total of 5 points.

ASSEMBLY

Using Star as pattern, cut piece magnetic canvas 1/8 inch smaller around outer edge. Attach to back of Star. ■

Fanciful Fruits

Cherries

SKILL LEVEL

FINISHED SIZE
2¼ x 2¾ inches

MATERIALS
- Aunt Lydia's Classic Crochet size 10 crochet cotton (350 yds per ball):
  15 yds #494 victory red
  5 yds #484 myrtle green
- Size 7/1.65mm steel crochet hook or size needed to obtain gauge
- Darice Magnetic Canvas:
  #1195-03 self-adhesive 5 x 8-inch sheet
- Spray starch

GAUGE
3 hdc = ¼ inch; 3 hdc rows = 5⁄16 inch

PATTERN NOTES
Chain-2 at beginning of round counts as first half double crochet unless otherwise stated.

Join with slip stitch as indicated unless otherwise stated.

INSTRUCTIONS
CHERRY
MAKE 3.
Rnd 1: With victory red, ch 2, 10 hdc in 2nd ch from hook, **join** *(see Pattern Notes)* in top of beg hdc. *(10 hdc)*

Rnd 2: Ch 2 *(see Pattern Notes)*, hdc in same st, 2 hdc in each st around, join in 2nd ch of beg ch-2. *(20 hdc)*

Rnd 3: Ch 2, hdc in same st, hdc in next st, [2 hdc in next st, hdc in next st] around, join in 2nd ch of beg ch-2. Fasten off. *(30 hdc)*

STEMS
For **first Stem**, with myrtle green, ch 11, sc in top of 1 Cherry, sl st in each of next 11 chs, **turn**, for **2nd stem**, ch 4, sc in top of next Cherry *(see photo)*, sl st in each of next 4 chs, sl st in top of first Stem, for **3rd Stem**, ch 4, sc in top of last Cherry, sl st in each of next 4 chs, sl st in end of first Stem.

LEAVES
For **first Leaf**, with myrtle green, *ch 6, sl st in 2nd ch from hook, sc in next ch, hdc in next ch, 2 hdc in each of last 2 chs, sl st in top of first Stem*, **turn**, for **2nd Leaf**, rep between * once. Fasten off.

ASSEMBLY
1. Spray Cherries, Stems and Leaves lightly with starch, shape; let dry.

2. Arrange Cherries into a cluster *(see photo)*, using cluster as pattern, cut piece magetic canvas ⅛ inch smaller around outer edge. Attach to back of Cherries. ■

Cluster of Grapes

SKILL LEVEL

EASY

FINISHED SIZE

1⅞ x 2½ inches

MATERIALS

- Aunt Lydia's Classic Crochet size 10 crochet cotton (350 yds per ball):
  - 15 yds #458 purple
  - 5 yds #484 myrtle green
- Sizes 10/1.15mm and 7/1.65mm steel crochet hooks or size needed to obtain gauge
- Tapestry needle
- Darice Magnetic Canvas:
  - #1195-03 self-adhesive 5 x 8-inch sheet
- Spray starch

GAUGE

Size 7 hook: 3 sc = ¼ inch; 2 sc rows = 5/16 inch

PATTERN NOTE

Join with slip stitch as indicated unless otherwise stated.

INSTRUCTIONS

GRAPE

MAKE 8.

Rnd 1: With size 7 hook and purple, ch 2, 8 sc in 2nd ch from hook, **join** *(see Pattern Note)* in beg sc. *(8 sc)*

Rnd 2: Ch 1, 2 sc in each st around, join in beg sc. Fasten off. *(16 sc)*

LEAF

With size 10 hook and myrtle green, ch 2, (sc, hdc, ch 2, sl st) 5 times in 2nd ch from hook. Fasten off.

ASSEMBLY

1. Spray Grapes and Leaf lightly with starch, shape; let dry.

2. Using 1 Grape as pattern, cut 8 pieces magnetic canvas ⅛ inch smaller around outer edge. Attach 1 to back of each Grape.

3. Arrange Grapes into a cluster *(see photo)*, tack tog.

4. Tack Leaf to top of cluster. ■

Lemon Wedge

SKILL LEVEL

EASY

FINISHED SIZE

7/8 x 2 inches

MATERIALS

- Aunt Lydia's Classic Crochet size 10 crochet cotton (white: 400 yds per ball; solids: 350 yds per ball):
  5 yds each #422 golden yellow
  and #1 white
- Size 7/1.65mm steel crochet hook or size needed to obtain gauge
- Darice Magnetic Canvas:
  #1195-03 self-adhesive 5 x 8-inch sheet
- Spray starch

GAUGE

3 hdc = 1/4 inch; 3 sc = 1/4 inch

PATTERN NOTE

Chain-2 at beginning of row counts as first half double crochet unless otherwise stated.

INSTRUCTIONS

LEMON WEDGE

Rnd 1: With white, ch 2, 5 sc in 2nd ch from hook, join with sl st in beg sc. Fasten off. *(5 sc)*

Row 2: Now working in rows, join golden yellow with sl st in first st, **ch 2** *(see Pattern Note)*, hdc in same st, hdc in **back lp** *(see Stitch Guide)* of next st, 2 hdc in next st, hdc in back lp of next st, 2 hdc in last st, turn. *(8 hdc)*

Row 3: Ch 2, hdc in same st, hdc each of next 3 sts, 2 hdc in next st, hdc in each of next 2 sts, 2 hdc in last st, turn. *(11 hdc)*

Row 4: Ch 2, hdc in same st, hdc in each of next 4 sts, 2 hdc in next st, hdc in each of next 4 sts, 2 hdc in last st, turn. Fasten off. *(14 hdc)*

Row 5: Working this row in back lps, join white with sc in first st, 2 sc in next st, sc in each of next 3 sts, tr in rem lp of next st on row 1, sc in next st on this row behind tr, sc in each of next 3 sts, tr in rem lp of next st on row 1, sc in next st on this row behind tr, sc in each of next 3 sts, 2 sc in last st. Fasten off. *(18 sts)*

Row 6: Working this row in back lps, join golden yellow with sl st in first st, ch 2, hdc in same st, hdc in each st across with 2 hdc in each tr and in last st. Fasten off.

ASSEMBLY

1. Spray Lemon Wedge lightly with starch, shape; let dry.

2. Using Lemon Wedge as pattern, cut piece magnetic canvas 1/8 inch smaller around outer edge. Attach to back of Lemon Wedge. ■

Orange Slice

SKILL LEVEL

EASY

FINISHED SIZE
1¾ inches in diameter

MATERIALS
- Aunt Lydia's Classic Crochet size 10 crochet cotton (white: 400 yds per ball; solids: 350 yds per ball):
  - 10 yds #431 pumpkin
  - 5 yds #1 white
- Size 7/1.65mm steel crochet hook or size needed to obtain gauge
- Darice Magnetic Canvas:
  - #1195-03 self-adhesive 5 x 8-inch sheet
- Spray starch

GAUGE
2 sc = ¼ inch; 2 sc rows = ¼ inch

PATTERN NOTE
Join with slip stitch as indicated unless otherwise stated.

INSTRUCTIONS
ORANGE SLICE
Rnd 1: With white, ch 2, 6 sc in 2nd ch from hook, **join** *(see Pattern Note)* in beg sc. Fasten off. *(6 sc)*

Rnd 2: Working this rnd in **back lps** *(see Stitch Guide)*, join pumpkin with sc in first st, sc in same st, 2 sc in each st around, join in beg sc. *(12 sc)*

Rnd 3: Ch 1, 2 sc in first st, sc in next st, [2 sc in next st, sc in next st] around, join in beg sc. *(18 sc)*

Rnd 4: Ch 1, 2 sc in first st, sc in each of next 2 sts, [2 sc in next st, sc in each of next 2 sts] around, join in beg sc. *(24 sc)*

Rnd 5: Ch 1, 2 sc in first st, sc in each of next 3 sts, [2 sc in next st, sc in each of next 3 sts] around, join in beg sc. Fasten off. *(30 sc)*

Rnd 6: Working this rnd in back lps, join white with sc in first st, sc in same st, tr in rem lp of corresponding st on rnd 1, sc in next st on last rnd behind tr, sc in each of next 3 sts, [2 sc in next st, tr in rem lp of next st on rnd 1, sc in next st on last rnd behind tr, sc in each of next 3 sts] around, join in beg sc. Fasten off. *(36 sc, 6 tr)*

Rnd 7: Working this rnd in back lps, join pumpkin with sc in any tr, sc in same st, sc in each st around with 2 sc in each tr, join in beg sc. Fasten off.

ASSEMBLY
1. Spray Orange Slice lightly with starch, shape; let dry.

2. Using Orange Slice as pattern, cut piece magnetic canvas ⅛ inch smaller around outer edge. Attach to back of Orange Slice. ■

Pineapple

SKILL LEVEL

EASY

FINISHED SIZE

1⅜ x 2¾ inches

MATERIALS

- Aunt Lydia's Classic Crochet size 10 crochet cotton (350 yds per ball):
  10 yds each #421 goldenrod
  5 yds #484 myrtle green
- Sizes 10/1.15mm and 7/1.65mm steel crochet hooks or size needed to obtain gauge
- Tapestry needle
- Darice Magnetic Canvas:
  #1195-03 self-adhesive 5 x 8-inch sheet
- Spray starch

GAUGE

Size 7 hook: 5 sc = ½ inch; 5 sc rows = ½ inch

INSTRUCTIONS

PINEAPPLE

Row 1: With size 7 hook and goldenrod, ch 6, sc in 2nd ch from hook and in each ch across, turn. *(5 sc)*

Rows 2–4: Ch 1, 2 sc in first st, sc in each st across with 2 sc in last st, turn. *(11 sc at end of last row)*

Rows 5–9: Ch 1, sc in each st across, turn.

Rows 10–13: Ch 1, **sc dec** *(see Stitch Guide)* in first 2 sts, sc in each st across to last 2 sts, sc dec in last 2 sts, turn. Fasten off at end of last row. *(3 sc at end of last row)*

TOP

With size 10 hook and myrtle green, join with sl st in 2nd st of row 13 on Pineapple, [ch 6, sl st in 2nd ch from hook and in each ch across, sl st in same st on row 13, ch 8, sl st in 2nd ch from hook and in each ch across, sl st in same st on row 13] twice, ch 4, sl st in 2nd ch from hook and in each ch across, sl st in same st on row 13, ch 3, sl st in 2nd ch from hook and last ch, sl st in same st on row 13. Fasten off.

ASSEMBLY

1. With goldenrod, using **straight stitch** *(see Fig. 1)*, embroider 4 long sts diagonally, evenly sp from right to left across Pineapple *(see photo)*. Working over sts just made, rep from left to right.

Fig. 1
Straight Stitch

2. Spray Pineapple lightly with starch, shape; let dry.

3. Using Pineapple as pattern, cut piece magnetic canvas ⅛ inch smaller around outer edge. Attach to back of Pineapple. ■

Feathered Friends

Bluebird

SKILL LEVEL

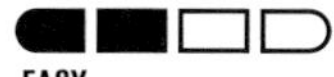

EASY

FINISHED SIZE
2 x 2½ inches

MATERIALS
- Aunt Lydia's Classic Crochet size 10 crochet cotton (350 yds per ball):
  15 yds each #480 delft
  2 yds #421 goldenrod
- Size 7/1.65mm steel crochet hook or size needed to obtain gauge
- Beading needle
- Darice Magnetic Canvas:
  #1195-03 self-adhesive 5 x 8-inch sheet
- 4mm round bead: 1 black
- Spray starch
- Black sewing thread
- Hot-glue gun

GAUGE
5 sc = ½ inch; 4 sc rows = ½ inch

PATTERN NOTE
Chain-2 at beginning of row counts as first half double crochet unless otherwise stated.

INSTRUCTIONS

BODY

Row 1: With delft, ch 10, hdc in 2nd ch from hook and in each ch across, turn. *(9 hdc)*

Rows 2–4: **Ch 2** *(see Pattern Note)*, hdc in same st, hdc in each st across with 2 hdc in last st, turn. *(15 hdc at end of last row)*

Row 5: Ch 2, hdc in each st across, turn.

Row 6: Ch 1, hdc in each st across to last 2 sts, **hdc dec** *(see Stitch Guide)* in last 2 sts, turn. *(14 hdc)*

Row 7: Ch 2, hdc dec in next 2 sts, hdc in each st across, turn. *(13 hdc)*

Row 8: For **head**, ch 2, hdc in same st, hdc in each of next 5 sts, hdc dec in next 2 sts, leaving rem sts unworked, turn. *(8 hdc)*

Row 9: Ch 2, hdc in each st across, turn.

Row 10: Ch 2, hdc dec in next 2 sts, hdc in each st across to last 2 sts, hdc dec in last 2 sts, turn. *(6 hdc)*

Row 11: Ch 2, hdc dec in next 2 sts, hdc in next st, hdc dec in last 2 sts. Fasten off.

BEAK

Join goldenrod with sl st in end of row 10 on Head, ch 2, (hdc, sl st) in same row. Fasten off.

TAIL

Row 1: Join delft with sl st in end of row 5 on Body at opposite side of Head, ch 2, hdc in end of each of next 2 rows, 2 hdc in next st on row 8, turn. *(5 hdc)*

Row 2: Ch 2, hdc in same st, hdc in each st across, turn. *(6 hdc)*

Rows 3 & 4: Ch 2, hdc in same st, hdc in each st across with 2 hdc in last st, turn. Fasten off at end of last row. *(10 hdc at end of last row)*

WING

Row 1: With delft, ch 6, sc in 2nd ch from hook and in each ch across, turn. *(5 sc)*

Rows 2–4: Ch 1, 2 sc in first st, sc in each st across with 2 sc in last st, turn. *(11 sc at end of last row)*

Row 5: Ch 1, sc in each of first 5 sts, **sc dec** *(see Stitch Guide)* in next 2 sts, leaving rem sts unworked, turn. *(6 sc)*

Row 6: Ch 1, sc dec in first 2 sts, sc in each of next 2 sts, sc dec in last 2 sts, turn. *(4 sc)*

Row 7: Ch 1, sc dec in first 2 sts, sc dec in last 2 sts. Fasten off.

ASSEMBLY

1. Spray Bluebird and Wing lightly with starch, shape; let dry.

2. Glue Wing to Body.

3. Sew bead to head 1/8 inch from Beak for eye.

4. Using Bluebird for pattern, cut piece magnetic canvas 1/8 inch smaller around outer edge. Attach to back of Bluebird. ■

Cardinal

SKILL LEVEL

EASY

FINISHED SIZE

1½ x 2½ inches

MATERIALS

- Aunt Lydia's Classic Crochet size 10 crochet cotton (350 yds per ball):
  15 yds #494 victory red
  2 yds each #421 goldenrod and #12 black
- Sizes 10/1.15mm and 7/1.65mm steel crochet hooks or size needed to obtain gauge
- Beading needle
- Darice Magnetic Canvas:
  #1195-03 self-adhesive 5 x 8-inch sheet
- 24-gauge wire: 1¾ inches black
- 2 black seed beads
- Spray starch
- Black sewing thread
- Hot-glue gun

GAUGE

Size 7 hook: 4 sc = ½ inch; 4 sc rows = ½ inch

INSTRUCTIONS

TAIL

Row 1: With size 7 hook and victory red, ch 7, sc in 2nd ch from hook and in each ch across, turn. *(6 sc)*

Rows 2–6: Working these rows in **back lps** *(see Stitch Guide)*, ch 1, sc in each st across, turn. **Do not turn** at end of last row.

BODY

Row 1: Working in ends of rows, ch 1, evenly sp 5 sc across, turn. *(5 sc)*

Rows 2–4: Ch 1, 2 sc in first st, sc in each st across with 2 sc in last st, turn. *(11 sc at end of last row)*

Rows 5–10: Ch 1, sc in each st across, turn.

Rows 11–14: Ch 1, **sc dec** *(see Stitch Guide)* in first 2 sts, sc in each st across to last 2 sts, sc dec in last 2 sts, turn. *(3 sc at end of last row)*

Row 15: Ch 1, sc dec in next 3 sts. Fasten off.

INNER BEAK

Row 1: With size 10 hook and black, ch 5, sc in 2nd ch from hook and in each ch across, turn. *(4 sc)*

Row 2: Ch 1, sc dec in first 2 sts, sc dec in last 2 sts, turn. *(2 sc)*

Row 3: Ch 1, sc dec in next 2 sts. Fasten off.

OUTER BEAK

With size 10 hook and goldenrod, ch 2, 3 hdc in 2nd ch from hook. Fasten off.

WING
MAKE 2.

With size 7 hook and victory red, ch 6, sl st in 2nd ch from hook, sl st in next ch, sc in next ch, hdc in next ch, 6 hdc in last ch, working on opposite side of ch, hdc in next ch, sc in next ch, sl st in each of last 2 chs, join with sl st in beg sl st. Fasten off.

ASSEMBLY

1. Spray Body, Beaks and Wings lightly with starch, shape; let dry.

2. Glue 1 Wing to each side of Body *(see photo)*.

3. Glue Outer Beak centered to Inner Beak. Glue Inner Beak centered over rows 10–12 of Body.

4. Sew beads to Body centered above Beak for eyes.

5. Place black wire across front of Body for perch. For each bird claw, with goldenrod, make 2 stitches ¼ inch apart around wire, tacking wire to Body *(see photo)*.

6. Using Cardinal for pattern, cut piece magnetic canvas ⅛ inch smaller around outer edge. Attach to back of Cardinal. ■

Eagle

SKILL LEVEL

EASY

FINISHED SIZE

2⅛ x 2⅛ inches

MATERIALS

- Aunt Lydia's Classic Crochet size 10 crochet cotton (white: 400 yds per ball; solids: 350 yds per ball):
  - 10 yds #12 black
  - 5 yds each #1 white, #131 fudge brown and #421 goldenrod
- Size 7/1.65mm steel crochet hook or size needed to obtain gauge
- Beading needle
- Darice Magnetic Canvas: #1195-03 self-adhesive 5 x 8-inch sheet
- 4mm round bead: 1 black
- Spray starch
- Black sewing thread
- Hot-glue gun

GAUGE

5 sc = ½ inch; 4 sc rows = ½ inch

PATTERN NOTE

Chain-2 at beginning of row counts as first half double crochet unless otherwise stated.

INSTRUCTIONS

BODY

Row 1: Starting at top of head, with white, ch 4, sc in 2nd ch from hook and in each ch across, turn. *(3 sc)*

Row 2: Ch 1, 2 sc in first st, sc in next st, 2 sc in last st, turn. *(5 sc)*

Rows 3–5: Ch 1, sc in each st across, turn. Fasten off at end of last row.

Row 6: For Body, working this row in **back lps** *(see Stitch Guide)*, join fudge brown with sc in first st, sc in each st across, turn.

Row 7: Ch 1, 2 sc in first st, sc in each st across with 2 sc in last st, turn. *(7 sc)*

Rows 8 & 9: Ch 1, sc in each st across, turn.

Row 10: Ch 1, **sc dec** *(see Stitch Guide)* in first 2 sts, sc in each st across to last 2 sts, sc dec in last 2 sts, turn. *(5 sc)*

Row 11: Ch 1, sc in each st across, turn.

Row 12: Ch 1, sc dec in first 2 sts, sc in next st, sc dec in last 2 sts. Fasten off.

WINGS

Row 1: With black, ch 16, hdc in 2nd ch from hook, hdc in each of next 4 chs, 2 hdc in next ch, hdc in each of next 3 chs, 2 hdc in next ch, hdc in each of last 5 chs, turn. *(17 hdc)*

Rows 2–4: **Ch 2** *(see Pattern Note)*, **hdc dec** *(see Stitch Guide)* in next 2 sts, hdc in each of next 3 sts, 2 hdc in next st, hdc in each of next 3 sts, 2 hdc in next st, hdc in each of next 4 sts, hdc dec in last 2 sts, turn.

FIRST WING TIP

Row 1: Ch 2, hdc in each of next 2 sts, sc in next st, sl st in next st, leaving rem sts unworked, turn. *(3 hdc, 1 sc)*

Row 2: Ch 2, hdc in next hdc, sl st in last st. Fasten off.

2ND WING TIP

Row 1: Join black with sl st in first st on opposite side of row 4 of Wings, rep row 1 of First Wing Tip.

Row 2: Rep row 2 of First Wing Tip.

TAIL

Row 1: Working in starting ch on opposite side of row 1 on Wings, sk first 6 chs, join black with sl st in next ch, ch 2, hdc in same ch, hdc in next ch, 2 hdc in next ch, leaving rem chs unworked, turn. *(5 hdc)*

Rows 2 & 3: Ch 2, hdc in same st, hdc in each st across with 2 hdc in last st, turn. Fasten off at end of last row. *(9 hdc at end of last row)*

BEAK

Join goldenrod with sl st in end of row 3 on right-hand side of Head, ch 3, sl st in 2nd ch from hook, sl st in next ch, sl st in same row as joining. Fasten off.

ASSEMBLY

1. Spray Body and Wings lightly with starch, shape; let dry.

2. With top of brown section on Body even with top of Wings, glue brown section of Body centered to top of Wings.

3. Sew bead to head one st from Beak for eye.

4. Using Eagle for pattern, cut piece magnetic canvas 1/8 inch smaller around outer edge. Attach to back of Eagle. ■

Hummingbird

SKILL LEVEL

EASY

FINISHED SIZE

2 1/8 x 4 inches

MATERIALS

- Aunt Lydia's Classic Crochet size 10 crochet cotton (white: 400 yds per ball; solids: 350 yds per ball):
  - 15 yds each #484 myrtle green and #661 frosty green
  - 5 yds each #431 pumpkin, #1 white and #12 black
- Sizes 10/1.15mm and 7/1.65mm steel crochet hooks or size needed to obtain gauge
- Beading needle
- Darice Magnetic Canvas: #1195-03 self-adhesive 5 x 8-inch sheet
- 4mm round bead: 1 black
- Spray starch
- Black sewing thread

GAUGE

Size 7 hook: 5 sc = 1/2 inch; 4 sc rows = 1/2 inch

PATTERN NOTE

Chain-2 at beginning of row counts as first half double crochet unless otherwise stated.

INSTRUCTIONS

HUMMINGBIRD

Row 1: With size 7 hook and frosty green, ch 2, 3 sc in 2nd ch from hook, turn. *(3 sc)*

Rows 2 & 3: Ch 1, sc in each st across, turn.

Row 4: Ch 1, 2 sc in first st, sc in next st, 2 sc in last st, turn. *(5 sc)*

Rows 5 & 6: Ch 1, sc in each st across, turn.

Row 7: Ch 1, 2 sc in first st, sc in each st across with 2 sc in last st, turn. *(7 sc)*

Rows 8–12: Ch 1, sc in each st across, turn. Fasten off at end of last row.

Row 13: Join white with sl st in first st, **ch 2** *(see Pattern Note)*, hdc in each of next 3 sts, sc in each of last 3 sts, turn. *(4 hdc, 3 sc)*

Row 14: Ch 1, sl st in each of first 2 sts, sc in each of next 2 sts, hdc in each of last 3 sts, turn. Fasten off.

Row 15: Join pumpkin with sl st in first st, ch 2, hdc in each of next 3 sts, sc in next st, **sc dec** *(see Stitch Guide)* in last 2 sts, turn. *(4 hdc, 2 sc)*

Row 16: Ch 2, **hdc dec** *(see Stitch Guide)* in next 2 sts, sc in each of last 3 sts, turn. *(3 sc, 2 hdc)*

Row 17: Ch 1, sc in each st across, turn. *(5 sc)*

Row 18: Ch 1, sc dec in first 2 sts, sc dec in next 2 sts, sc in last st. Fasten off. *(3 sc)*

BEAK

With size 10 hook and black, join with sl st in first st of row 18 on right-hand side, ch 10, sl st in 2nd ch from hook and in each ch across, sl st in same st first sl st. Fasten off.

UPPER BODY

Row 1: With size 7 hook and myrtle green, join with sl st in same st as Beak was worked in, evenly sp 6 sc around pumpkin section of head to white section on neck, evenly sp 2 sc across white neck section, evenly sp 12 sc across body to row 1, ch 8, turn. *(20 sc, 8 chs)*

Row 2: For **tail**, hdc in 2nd ch from hook and in each of next 3 chs, sc in each of next 2 chs, sl st in last ch, sl st in next sc, leaving rem sts unworked. Fasten off.

FIRST WING

Row 1: With size 7 hook and myrtle green, join with sl st in 9th st on row 1 of Upper Body, ch 2, 2 hdc in same st, 3 hdc in back lp of next st, leaving rem sts unworked, turn. *(6 hdc)*

Rows 2–5: Ch 2, hdc in each st across, turn.

Row 6: Ch 2, hdc dec in next 2 sts, hdc in next st, hdc dec in last 2 sts, turn. *(4 hdc)*

Row 7: Ch 2, hdc dec in last 2 sts. Fasten off.

2ND WING

Row 1: With RS facing, join with sl st in rem **front lp** *(see Stitch Guide)* of 10 st on Upper Body, ch 2, 2 hdc in next st, 3 hdc in next st leaving rem sts unworked, turn. *(6 hdc)*

Rows 2–7: Rep rows 2–7 of First Wing.

ASSEMBLY

1. Spray Bird lightly with starch, shape; let dry.

2. Sew bead to row 17 of Bird for eye *(see photo)*.

3. Using Hummingbird for pattern, cut piece magnetic canvas ⅛ inch smaller around outer edge. Attach to back of Bird. ■

Peacock

SKILL LEVEL

EASY

FINISHED SIZE

2¼ x 3½ inches

MATERIALS

- Aunt Lydia's Classic Crochet size 10 crochet cotton (350 yds per ball):
  20 yds #397 wasabi
  10 yds each #487 dark royal and #451 parakeet
- Size 7/1.65mm steel crochet hook or size needed to obtain gauge
- Beading needle
- Darice Magnetic Canvas: #1195-03 self-adhesive 5 x 8-inch sheet
- 1 black seed bead
- Spray starch
- Black sewing thread
- Hot-glue gun

GAUGE

5 hdc = ½ inch; 4 hdc rows = ½ inch

PATTERN NOTE

Chain-2 at beginning of row counts as first half double crochet unless otherwise stated.

SPECIAL STITCH

Cluster (cl): Ch 2, [yo, insert hook in same row, yo, pull lp through, yo, pull through 2 lps on hook] twice, yo, pull through all 3 lps on hook.

INSTRUCTIONS

BODY

Row 1: With parakeet, ch 6, sc in 2nd ch from hook and in each ch across, turn. *(5 sc)*

Rows 2 & 3: **Ch 2** *(see Pattern Note)*, hdc in same st, hdc in each st across with 2 hdc last st, turn. *(9 hdc at end of last row)*

Rows 4 & 5: Ch 2, hdc in each st across, turn.

Rows 6 & 7: Ch 2, **hdc dec** *(see Stitch Guide)* in next 2 sts, hdc in each st across to last 2 sts, hdc dec in last 2 sts, turn. *(5 hdc at end of last row)*

Row 8: Ch 2, hdc in each of next 2 sts, hdc dec in last 2 sts, turn. *(4 dc)*

Rows 9–11: Ch 2, hdc in each st across, turn. Fasten off at end of last row.

BEAK

Join dark royal with sl st in end of row 10 on right-hand side of Body, (ch 2, hdc, ch 1, sl st) in same row. Fasten off.

TAIL

Row 1: With wasabi, ch 12, hdc in 2nd ch from hook and in each of next 3 chs, sc in each of next 4 chs, sl st in each of last 3 chs, turn. *(11 sts)*

Row 2: Ch 1, sl st in each of first 3 sts, sc in each of next 4 sts, hdc in each of last 4 sts, turn.

Row 3: Working this row in **back lps** *(see Stitch Guide)*, ch 2, hdc in each of next 3 sts, sc in each of next 4 sts, sl st in each of last 3 sts, turn.

Rows 4–29: [Rep rows 2 and 3 alternately] 13 times.

Row 30: Rep row 2. Fasten off.

Row 31: Join dark royal with sl st in end of row 3, **cl** *(see Special Stitch)*, [sk next row, sl st in next row, cl] 14 times. Fasten off.

Row 32: Join wasabi with sl st in end of row 1 of Tail, (sc, hdc, ch 1, hdc, sc) in next cl, [sl st in sp between worked cl and next cl, (sc, hdc, ch 1, hdc, sc) in next cl] across, sl st in end of last row of Tail. Fasten off.

ASSEMBLY

1. Spray Body and Tail lightly with starch, shape; let dry.

2. Sew bead to head one st from Beak for eye.

3. With parakeet, using **straight stitch** *(see Fig. 1)*, embroider one st at top and each side of each cluster.

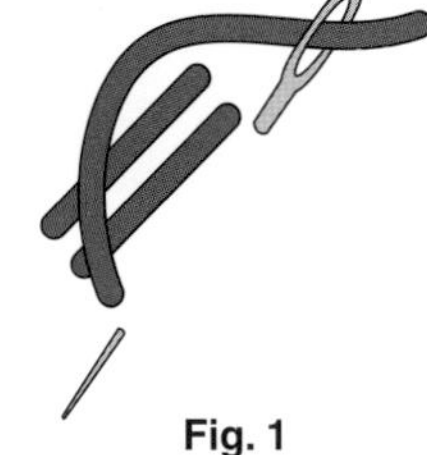

Fig. 1
Straight Stitch

4. Weave strand wasabi through ends of rows on Tail opposite clusters, pull to gather slightly to form ½ circle. Secure end.

5. With bottom of Body even with Bottom of Tail, glue Body centered to Tail.

6. Using Peacock for pattern, cut piece magnetic canvas ⅛ inch smaller around outer edge. Attach to back of Peacock. ■

Glamour Girl

Lipstick

SKILL LEVEL

EASY

FINISHED SIZE

⅞ x 2¾ inches

MATERIALS

- Kreinik Metallics #16 medium braid (11 yds/10m per spool):
  1 spool #001HL silver hi lustre
- Aunt Lydia's Classic Crochet size 10 crochet cotton (350 yds per ball):
  5 yds #494 victory red
- Size 7/1.65mm steel crochet hook or size needed to obtain gauge
- Darice Magnetic Canvas:
  #1195-03 self-adhesive 5 x 8-inch sheet

GAUGE

4 sc = ½ inch; 4 sc rows = ½ inch

INSTRUCTIONS

LIPSTICK

Row 1: With silver, ch 7, sc in 2nd ch from hook and in each ch across, turn. *(6 sc)*

Rows 2–12: Ch 1, sc in each st across, turn. At end of last row, **do not turn**. Fasten off.

Row 13: Sk first st, join victory red with sc in next st, sc in each of next 3 sts, leaving rem sts unworked, turn. *(4 sc)*

Rows 14–17: Ch 1, sc in each st across, turn.

Row 18: Ch 1, sk first st, sc in each st across, turn. *(3 sc)*

Row 19: Ch 1, sc in first st, **sc dec** *(see Stitch Guide)* in last 2 sts, turn. *(2 sc)*

Row 20: Ch 1, sk first st, sc in last st. Fasten off

ASSEMBLY

Using Lipstick as pattern, cut piece magnetic canvas ⅛ inch smaller around outer edge. Attach to back of Lipstick. ■

High Heel

SKILL LEVEL

EASY

FINISHED SIZE

1¾ x 1⁵⁄₁₆ inches

MATERIALS

- Kreinik Metallics #16 medium braid (11 yds/10m per spool):
  1 spool #003HL red hi lustre
- Size 7/1.65mm steel crochet hook or size needed to obtain gauge
- Darice Magnetic Canvas:
  #1195-03 self-adhesive 5 x 8-inch sheet

GAUGE

4 sc = ½ inch; 4 sc rows = ½ inch

INSTRUCTIONS

HIGH HEEL

Row 1: Ch 8, sc in 2nd ch from hook and in each of next 5 chs, 2 sc in last ch, turn. *(8 sc)*

Row 2: Ch 1, 2 sc in first st, sc in each sc across to last 2 sts, **sc dec** *(see Stitch Guide)* in last 2 sts, turn.

Row 3: Ch 1, sk first st, sc in each st across with 2 sc in last st, turn.

Row 4: Ch 1, 2 sc in first st, sc in each of next 2 sts, sc dec in next 2 sts, leaving rem sts uworked, turn. *(5 sc)*

Row 5: Ch 1, sk first st, sc in each of next 3 sts, 2 sc in last st, turn.

Row 6: Ch 1, 2 sc in first st, sc in each of next 2 sts, sc dec in last 2 sts, turn.

Row 7: Ch 1, sk first st, sc in each of next 3 sts, 2 sc in last st, turn.

Row 8: Ch 1, sc in each of first 3 sts, sc dec in last 2 sts, turn. *(4 sc)*

Row 9: Ch 1, sk first st, sc in each st across, **do not turn**. *(3 sc)*

Row 10: Working in ends of rows, ch 1, sc in end of first row, 2 sc in next row, turn.

Row 11: For **Heel**, ch 8, sc in 2nd ch from hook and in each of next 6 chs, sl st in next st. Fasten off.

ASSEMBLY

Using High Heel as pattern, cut piece magnetic canvas ⅛ inch smaller around outer edge. Attach to back of High Heel. ■

Ring Bling

SKILL LEVEL

EASY

FINISHED SIZE

1 x 1½ inches

MATERIALS

- Kreinik Metallics #16 medium braid (11 yds/10m per spool):
  1 spool each #003HL red hi lustre and #001HL silver hi lustre

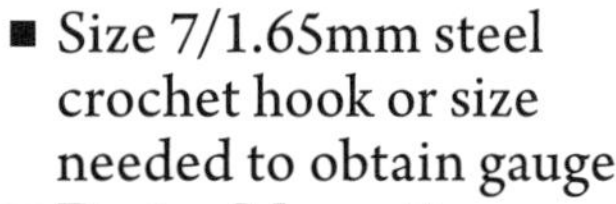

- Size 7/1.65mm steel crochet hook or size needed to obtain gauge
- Darice Magnetic Canvas:
  #1195-03 self-adhesive 5 x 8-inch sheet

GAUGE

5 sc = ½ inch; 3 sc rows = ¼ inch

INSTRUCTIONS
RING

Rnd 1: With silver, ch 14, sl st in beg ch to form ring, ch 1, 2 sc in each ch around, join with sl st in beg sc. Fasten off. *(28 sc)*

Row 2: Now working in rows, and this row in **back lps** *(see Stitch Guide)*, join red with sc in any st, sc in same st, sc in next st, 2 sc in next st, leaving rem sts unworked, turn. *(5 sc)*

Row 3: Ch 1, sc in each st across, turn.

Row 4: Ch 1, sc in each of first 4 sts, 2 sc in last st. Fasten off.

ASSEMBLY

Using Ring as pattern, cut piece magnetic canvas ⅛ inch smaller around outer edge and inner circle. Attach to back of Ring. ■

Purse

SKILL LEVEL

EASY

FINISHED SIZE

1½ x 2 inches

MATERIALS

- Kreinik Metallics #16 medium braid (11 yds/10m per spool):
  1 spool #003HL red hi lustre
- Size 7/1.65mm steel crochet hook or size needed to obtain gauge
- Darice Magnetic Canvas:
  #1195-03 self-adhesive 5 x 8-inch sheet
- Beading needle
- 4mm round beads: 19 black
- 26-gauge wire: 3 inches black
- Black sewing thread

GAUGE

4 sc = ½ inch; 4 sc rows = ½ inch

INSTRUCTIONS
PURSE

Row 1: Starting at lower edge, ch 11, sc in 2nd ch from hook and in each ch across, turn. *(10 sc)*

Rows 2–4: Ch 1, sc in each st across, turn.

Row 5: Ch 1, sk first st, sc in each st across to last 2 sts, **sc dec** *(see Stitch Guide)* in last 2 sts, turn. *(8 sc)*

Row 6: Ch 1, sc in each st across, turn.

Rows 7–10: [Rep rows 5 and 6 alternately] twice. *(4 sc at end of last row)*

Row 11: Ch 1, sc in each st across. Fasten off.

ASSEMBLY

1. Thread 15 beads onto wire. Bend wire into handle shape and attach 1 end to top left corner of Purse and opposite end to top right corner.

2. Sew 4 beads centered to front of Purse ¼ inch from top edge *(see photo)*.

3. Using Purse as pattern, cut piece magnetic canvas ⅛ inch smaller around outer edge. Attach to back of Purse. ■

Martini Glass

SKILL LEVEL

EASY

FINISHED SIZE

2 3/8 x 2 7/8 inches

MATERIALS

- Aunt Lydia's Classic Crochet size 10 crochet cotton (white: 400 yds per ball; solids: 350 yds per ball):
  10 yds #1 white
  2 yds each #901 pagoda red and #661 frosty green
- Size 7/1.65mm steel crochet hook or size needed to obtain gauge
- Darice Magnetic Canvas: #1195-03 self-adhesive 5 x 8-inch sheet
- 24-gauge wire: 1½ inches black
- Hot-glue gun

GAUGE

4 sc = ½ inch; 4 sc rows = ½ inch

INSTRUCTIONS

GLASS

Rnd 1: For **base**, with white, ch 12, sc in 2nd ch from hook and in each of next 9 chs, 3 sc in last ch, working on opposite side of ch, sc in each of next 9 chs, 2 sc in last ch, join with sl st in beg sc. Fasten off. *(24 sc)*

Row 2: For **stem**, now working in rows, working over sts into starting ch, join with sc in ch below 3rd st of first 9-sc group, working over sts, sc in each of next 3 chs of starting ch, turn. *(4 sc)*

Rows 3–12: Ch 1, sc in each st across, turn.

Rows 13–20: Ch 1, 2 sc in first st, sc in each st across with 2 sc in last st, turn. Fasten off at end of last row. *(20 sc at end of last row)*

OLIVE

Rnd 1: With pagoda red, ch 2, 5 sc in 2nd ch from hook, join with sl st in beg sc. Fasten off. *(5 sc)*

Rnd 2: Join frosty green with sl st in any st, 2 sc in next st, 2 hdc in each of next 2 sts, 2 sc in last st, join with sl st in beg sl st, turn. *(4 hdc, 4 sc)*

Row 3: Now working in rows, ch 2 *(counts as first hdc)*, hdc in each of next 2 sts, 2 hdc in next st, hdc in each of next 3 sts, leaving rem sts unworked, turn. *(8 hdc)*

Row 4: Ch 2, hdc in each of next 6 sts. Fasten off.

ASSEMBLY

1. Spray Glass and Olive lightly with starch, shape. Let dry.

2. Glue bottom half of Olive behind top rim of Glass *(see photo)*.

3. Leaving ½ inch straight, wrap wire around end of crochet hook to curl. Insert straight end into Olive and glue in place.

4. Using Martini Glass as pattern, cut piece magnetic canvas ⅛ inch smaller around outer edge. Attach to back of Martini Glass. ■

Patriotic Pride

Firecracker

SKILL LEVEL

EASY

FINISHED SIZE
7/8 x 1 3/4 inches

MATERIALS
- Aunt Lydia's Classic Crochet size 10 crochet cotton (white: 400 yds per ball; solids: 350 yds per ball):
  10 yds each #494 victory red and #487 dark royal
  5 yds #1 white
- Kreinik Metallics #16 medium braid (11 yds/10m per spool):
  1 spool #001HL silver hi lustre
- Size 7/1.65mm steel crochet hook or size needed to obtain gauge
- Tapestry needle
- Darice Magnetic Canvas:
  #1195-03 self-adhesive 5 x 8-inch sheet
- Spray starch

GAUGE
4 hdc = 1/2 inch; 4 hdc rows = 1/2 inch

INSTRUCTIONS
FIRECRACKER

Row 1: With dark royal, ch 9, sc in 2nd ch from hook and in each ch across, turn. *(8 sc)*

Rows 2 & 3: Ch 1, sc in each st across, turn. Fasten off at end of last row.

Row 4: Join white with sc in first st, sc in each st across, turn. Fasten off.

Row 5: Join victory red with sc in first st, sc in each st across, turn.

Rows 6–8: Ch 1, sc in each st across, turn. Fasten off at end of last row.

Row 9: Rep row 4.

Row 10: Join dark royal with sc in first st, sc in each st across, turn.

Rows 11 & 12: Ch 1, sc in each st across, turn. Fasten off at end of last row.

ASSEMBLY

1. Spray firecracker lightly with starch, shape; let dry.

2. With white, using **straight stitch** *(see Fig. 1)*, embroider 2 starbursts on Firecacker according to Embroidery Diagram *(see photo)*.

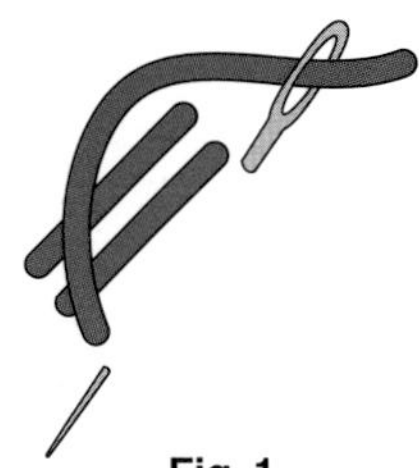

Fig. 1
Straight Stitch

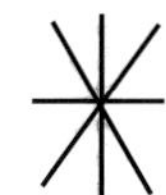

Firecracker
Starburst Embroidery Diagram

3. Cut strand silver 3 inches long, fold in half. Insert hook in back of center st at top of Firecracker, pull fold through, pull loose ends through fold. Separate strands for spark of Firecracker. Trim.

4. Using Firecracker as pattern, cut piece magnetic canvas 1/8 inch smaller around outer edge. Attach to back of Firecracker. ■

Heart Flag

SKILL LEVEL

EASY

FINISHED SIZE
1¾ x 1¾ inches

MATERIALS

- Aunt Lydia's Classic Crochet size 10 crochet cotton (white: 400 yds per ball; solids: 350 yds per ball):
  5 yds each #494 victory red, #1 white and #487 dark royal
- Size 7/1.65mm steel crochet hook or size needed to obtain gauge
- Tapestry needle
- Darice Magnetic Canvas:
  #1195-03 self-adhesive 5 x 8-inch sheet
- Spray starch

GAUGE
4 sc = ½ inch; 4 sc rows = ½ inch

INSTRUCTIONS
FLAG
Row 1: With victory red, ch 2, 3 sc in 2nd ch from hook, turn. *(3 sc)*

Row 2: Ch 1, 2 sc in first st, sc in next st, 2 sc in last st, turn. *(5 sc)*

Row 3: Ch 1, sc in each st across, turn. Fasten off.

Row 4: Join white with sc in first st, sc in same st, sc in each st across with 2 sc in last st, turn. *(7 sc)*

Row 5: Ch 1, sc in each st across, turn. Fasten off.

Rows 6 & 7: With victory red, rep rows 4 and 5. *(9 sc)*

Row 8: Rep row 4. *(11 sc)*

Row 9: Ch 1, 2 sc in first st, sc in each st across with 2 sc in last st, turn. Fasten off. *(13 sc)*

Row 10: Join victory red with sc in first st, sc in each of next 5 sts, **changing color** *(see Stitch Guide)* to dark royal in last st, sc in each of last 7 sts, turn.

Row 11: Ch 1, 2 sc in first st, sc in each of next 6 sts, changing to victory red in last st, sc in each of next 5 sts, 2 sc in last st, turn. Fasten off. *(15 sts)*

Row 12: Join white with sc in first st, sc in each of next 6 sts, changing to dark royal in last st, sc in each of last 8 sts, turn.

Row 13: Ch 1, sc in each of first 8 sts, changing to white in last st, sc in each of last 7 sts, turn. Fasten off.

FIRST SIDE
Row 1: Join victory red with sl st in first st, ch 1, **sc dec** *(see Stitch Guide)* in first 2 sts, sc in each of next 4 sts, sc dec in next 2 sts, leaving rem sts unworked, turn. *(6 sc)*

Row 2: Ch 1, sc dec in first 2 sts, sc in each of next 2 sts, sc dec in last 2 sts, turn. *(4 sc)*

Row 3: Ch 1, sc dec in first 2 sts, sc dec in last 2 sts. Fasten off.

2ND SIDE

Row 1: Join dark royal with sl st in last worked st on row 13 of Flag at center of heart, ch 1, sc dec in same st and next st, sc in each of next 4 sts, sc dec in last 2 sts, turn. *(6 sc)*

Rows 2 & 3: Rep rows 2 and 3 of First Side.

ASSEMBLY

1. Spray Flag lightly with starch, shape; let dry.

2. With white, using **straight stitch** *(see Fig. 1)*, embroider star on dark royal section according to Embroidery Diagram.

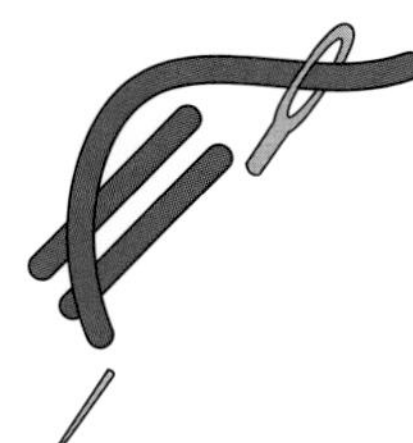

Fig. 1
Straight Stitch

Heart Flag
Star Embroidery Diagram

3. Using Flag as pattern, cut piece magnetic canvas 1/8 inch smaller around outer edge. Attach to back of Flag. ■

Red, White & Blue Stars

SKILL LEVEL

EASY

FINISHED SIZE

1 3/8 x 1 3/8 inches

MATERIALS

- Aunt Lydia's Classic Crochet size 10 crochet cotton (white: 400 yds per ball; solids: 350 yds per ball):
  5 yds each #494 victory red, #1 white and #487 dark royal
- Size 7/1.65mm steel crochet hook or size needed to obtain gauge
- Darice Magnetic Canvas: #1195-03 self-adhesive 5 x 8-inch sheet
- Spray starch

GAUGE

Rnds 1 and 2 = 1/2 inch across

PATTERN NOTE

Join with slip stitch as indicated unless otherwise stated.

INSTRUCTIONS

STAR

MAKE 1 OF EACH COLOR.

Rnd 1: Ch 2, 10 sc in 2nd ch from hook, **join** *(see Pattern Note)* in beg sc. *(10 sc)*

Rnd 2: Ch 1, 2 sc in each st around, join in beg sc. *(20 sc)*

Rnd 3: Ch 1, (sc, hdc) in first st, (dc, tr, ch 1, tr, dc) in next st, (hdc, sc) in next st, sl st in next st, *(sc, hdc) in next st, (dc, tr, ch 1, tr, dc) in next st, (hdc, sc) in next st, sl st in next st, rep from * around, join in beg sc. Fasten off.

ASSEMBLY

1. Spray Stars lightly with starch, shape; let dry.

2. For each Star, using Star as pattern, cut piece magnetic canvas 1/8 inch smaller around outer edge. Attach to back of Star. ■

Uncle Sam Hat

SKILL LEVEL

EASY

FINISHED SIZE

1⅝ x 1¾ inches

MATERIALS

- Aunt Lydia's Classic Crochet size 10 crochet cotton (white: 400 yds per ball; solids: 350 yds per ball):
  5 yds each #494 victory red, #1 white and #487 dark royal
- Size 7/1.65mm steel crochet hook or size needed to obtain gauge
- Darice Magnetic Canvas:
  #1195-03 self-adhesive 5 x 8-inch sheet
- Spray starch

GAUGE

4 sc = ½ inch; 4 sc rows = ½ inch

INSTRUCTIONS

HAT

Row 1: With victory red, ch 8, sc in 2nd ch from hook and in each ch across, turn. *(7 sc)*

Row 2: Join white with sc in first st, sc in each st across, turn. Fasten off.

Row 3: Join victory red with sc in first st, sc in each st across, turn. Fasten off.

Rows 4 & 5: Rep rows 2 and 3.

Row 6: Working in ends of rows at 1 end, join dark royal with sc in first row, sc in each row across, turn. *(5 sc)*

Rows 7 & 8: Ch 1, sc in each st across, turn. Fasten off at end of last row.

Row 9: For **brim**, with victory red, ch 4, join with sc in first st, sc in each st across, ch 5, turn. *(5 sc, 9 chs)*

Row 10: Sc in 2nd ch from hook, sc in each of next 3 chs, sc in each st across, sc in each of last 4 chs, turn. *(13 sc)*

Row 11: Ch 1, sc in each st across. Fasten off.

ASSEMBLY

1. Spray Hat lightly with starch, shape; let dry.

2. Using Hat as pattern, cut piece magnetic canvas ⅛ inch smaller around outer edge. Attach to back of Hat. ■

USA Sign

SKILL LEVEL

EASY

FINISHED SIZE
3 x 1½ inches

MATERIALS
- Aunt Lydia's Classic Crochet size 10 crochet cotton (white: 400 yds per ball; solids: 350 yds per ball):
  10 yds #480 delft
  5 yds each #494 victory red, #1 white and #487 dark royal
- Size 7/1.65mm steel crochet hook or size needed to obtain gauge
- Darice Magnetic Canvas:
  #1195-03 self-adhesive 5 x 8-inch sheet
- Spray starch
- Hot-glue gun

GAUGE
4 hdc = ½ inch; 3 hdc rows = ½ inch

PATTERN NOTE
Chain-2 at beginning of row counts as first half double crochet unless otherwise stated.

INSTRUCTIONS
LETTERS
MAKE 1 EACH VICTORY RED, WHITE AND DARK ROYAL.
Ch 18, sc in 2nd ch from hook and in each ch across. Fasten off.

"A" SHORT SECTION
With dark royal, ch 4, sc in 2nd ch from hook and in each ch across. Fasten off.

SIGN
Row 1: With delft, ch 12, hdc in 2nd ch from hook and in each ch across, turn. *(11 hdc)*

Rows 2–16: Ch 2 *(see Pattern Note)*, hdc in each st across, turn.

Rnd 17: Now working in rnds around entire outer edge, ch 1, sc in each st and in end of each row around with ch 1 in each corner, join with sl st in beg sc. Fasten off.

ASSEMBLY
1. Spray Letters and Sign lightly with starch, shape victory red Letter into a "U" shape, white Letter into an "S" shape and dark royal Letter into an "A" shape; let dry.

2. Glue Letters and "A" Short Section to Sign according to photo.

3. Using Sign as pattern, cut piece magnetic canvas ⅛ inch smaller around outer edge. Attach to back of Sign. ■

Pet Projects

Dog

SKILL LEVEL

EASY

FINISHED SIZE
1½ x 1¾ inches

MATERIALS
- Aunt Lydia's Classic Crochet size 10 crochet cotton (350 yds per ball):
  10 yds #210 antique white
  5 yds #12 black
- Size 7/1.65mm steel crochet hook or size needed to obtain gauge
- Beading needle
- Darice Magnetic Canvas: #1195-03 self-adhesive 5 x 8-inch sheet
- 4mm round beads: 2 black
- 8mm acrylic cabochon: 1 black
- Face blush
- Spray starch
- Black sewing thread
- Hot-glue gun

GAUGE
4 hdc = ½ inch; 4 hdc rows = ½ inch

PATTERN NOTE
Chain-2 at beginning of row counts as first half double crochet unless otherwise stated.

INSTRUCTIONS

FACE

Row 1: With antique white, ch 11, hdc in 2nd ch from hook and in each ch across, turn. *(10 hdc)*

Rows 2–6: **Ch 2** *(see Pattern Note)*, hdc in each st across, turn.

Rows 7–9: Ch 2, **hdc dec** *(see Stitch Guide)* in next 2 sts, hdc in each st across to last 2 sts, hdc dec in last 2 sts, turn. Fasten off at end of last row. *(4 hdc in last row)*

EAR
MAKE 2.

Row 1: With black, ch 5, hdc in 2nd ch from hook and in each ch across, turn. *(4 hdc)*

Rows 2–4: Ch 2, hdc in each st across, turn.

Row 5: Ch 2, **sc dec** *(see Stitch Guide)* in last 3 sts. Fasten off.

ASSEMBLY

1. Spray Face and Ears lightly with starch, shape; let dry.

2. Sew beads side-by-side centered on Face between rows 4 and 5 for eyes.

3. Glue cabochon to Face centered on row 2 for nose.

4. Glue Ears to each side of Face.

5. Brush cheeks of Face with blush.

6. Using Face as pattern, cut piece magnetic canvas ⅛ inch smaller around outer edge. Attach to back of Face. ■

Frog

SKILL LEVEL

EASY

FINISHED SIZE

1¾ x 2 inches

MATERIALS

- Aunt Lydia's Classic Crochet size 10 crochet cotton (white: 400 yds per ball; solids: 350 yds per ball):
  - 10 yds #397 wasabi
  - 2 yds each #1 white and #12 black
- Size 7/1.65mm steel crochet hook or size needed to obtain gauge
- Tapestry needle
- Beading needle
- Darice Magnetic Canvas: #1195-03 self-adhesive 5 x 8-inch sheet
- 8mm faceted round beads: 2 black
- Face blush
- Spray starch
- Black sewing thread
- Hot-glue gun

GAUGE

4 hdc = ½ inch; 3 hdc rows = ½ inch

PATTERN NOTE

Chain-2 at beginning of row counts as first half double crochet unless otherwise stated.

INSTRUCTIONS

BODY

Row 1: With wasabi, ch 11, hdc in 2nd ch from hook and in each ch across, turn. *(10 hdc)*

Rows 2–7: **Ch 2** *(see Pattern Note)*, hdc in each st across, turn.

Rows 8–10: Ch 2, **hdc dec** *(see Stitch Guide)* in next 2 sts, hdc in each st across to last 2 sts, hdc dec in last 2 sts, turn. Fasten off at end of last row. *(4 hdc in last row)*

EYEBALL

MAKE 2.

With white, ch 2, 10 sc in 2nd ch from hook, join with sl st in beg sc. Fasten off.

LEG

MAKE 2.

Row 1: Starting at **toes**, with wasabi, ch 2, 6 dc in 2nd ch from hook, **do not turn**. *(6 dc)*

Row 2: Ch 2, hdc in end of dc row, working on opposite side of ch, hdc in first ch, leaving rem chs unworked, turn. *(3 hdc)*

Rows 3–7: For **Legs**, ch 2, hdc in each st across, turn. Fasten off at end of last row.

ASSEMBLY

1. Spray Body, Eyeballs and Legs lightly with starch, shape; let dry.
2. Sew 1 bead to each Eyeball.
3. Glue Eyeballs side by side to top of Body. Glue 1 Leg to each side of Body with toes pointing out.
4. With black, using **backstitch** *(see Fig. 1)*, embroider mouth over rows 3–7 of Body as shown in photo.

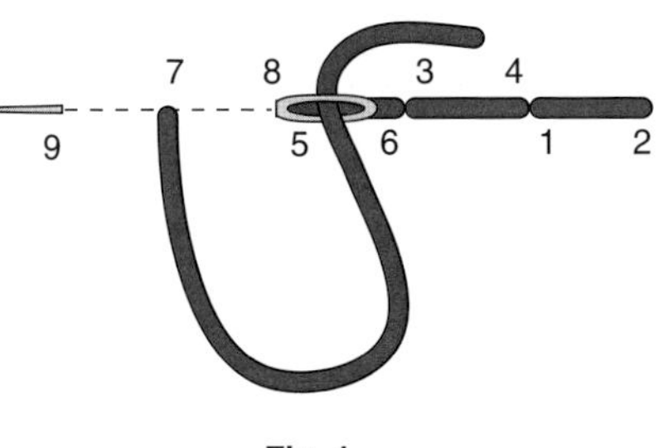

Fig. 1
Backstitch

5. Brush cheeks of Frog with blush.
6. Using Frog as pattern, cut piece magnetic canvas ⅛ inch smaller around outer edge. Attach to back of Frog. ■

Horse

SKILL LEVEL

EASY

FINISHED SIZE

1¾ x 2¼ inches

MATERIALS

- Aunt Lydia's Classic Crochet size 10 crochet cotton (white: 400 yds per ball; solids: 350 yds per ball):
  - 10 yds #310 copper mist
  - 5 yds each #1 white and #494 victory red
- Sizes 10/1.15mm and 7/1.65mm steel crochet hooks or size needed to obtain gauge
- Tapestry needle
- Beading needle
- Darice Magnetic Canvas:
  - #1195-03 self-adhesive 5 x 8-inch sheet
- 4mm round bead: 1 black
- Spray starch
- Black sewing thread

GAUGE

Size 7 hook: 4 hdc = ½ inch; 3 hdc rows = ½ inch

PATTERN NOTE

Chain-2 at beginning of row counts as first half double crochet unless otherwise stated.

INSTRUCTIONS

HORSE

Row 1: Starting at bottom of neck, with size 7 hook and copper mist, ch 10, hdc in 2nd ch from hook and in each ch across, turn. *(9 hdc)*

Row 2: **Ch 2** *(see Pattern Note)*, hdc in each st across to last 2 sts, **hdc dec** *(see Stitch Guide)* in last 2 sts, turn. *(8 hdc)*

Rows 3 & 4: Ch 2, hdc dec in next 2 sts, hdc in each st across, turn. *(6 hdc at end of last row)*

Rows 5 & 6: Rep rows 2 and 3. *(4 hdc at end of last row)*

Row 7: Ch 2, hdc in next st, hdc dec in last 2 sts, turn. *(3 hdc)*

Row 8: Ch 2, hdc dec in last 2 sts turn. *(2 hdc)*

Row 9: Ch 2, hdc in last st, turn.

Row 10: For **head**, ch 2, hdc in same st, hdc in last st, working in ends of rows, hdc in end of each of next 4 rows, turn. *(7 hdc)*

Row 11: Ch 2, hdc in same st, hdc in each st across, turn. *(8 hdc)*

Row 12: Ch 2, hdc in each st across with 2 hdc in last st, turn. *(9 hdc)*

Row 13: Ch 2, hdc dec in next 2 sts, hdc in each st across, turn. *(8 hdc)*

Row 14: Ch 3, for **ear**, (dc, hdc, sl st) in same st, leaving rem sts unworked. Fasten off.

MANE

Working in ends of rows across back of neck *(see photo)*, with size 7 hook and white, join with sl st in end of row 1, ch 5, sl st in same row, evenly sp sts, (ch 5, sl st) 13 times across to base of ear, drop lp from hook, insert hook in st on opposite side of ear, pull dropped lp through, [ch 3, sl st in same sp] twice, ch 3, [sl st, ch 3, sl st] in next row. Fasten off.

SHORT BRIDAL

With size 10 hook and victory red, ch 5. Fasten off.

LONG BRIDAL

With size 10 hook and victory red, ch 10. Fasten off.

ASSEMBLY

1. Tack Short Bridal across nose of head and Long Bridal from nose to back of ear.

2. Spray Horse lightly with starch, shape; let dry.

3. For **eye**, sew bead to row 12 of head 1/4 inch from ear.

4. Using Horse as pattern, cut piece magnetic canvas 1/8 inch smaller around outer edge. Attach to back of Horse. ■

Kitty

SKILL LEVEL

EASY

FINISHED SIZE

1¼ x 2 inches

MATERIALS

- Aunt Lydia's Classic Crochet size 10 crochet cotton (white: 400 yds per ball; solids: 350 yds per ball):
  - 10 yds #423 maize
  - 2 yds each #1 white and #493 French rose
- Size 7/1.65mm steel crochet hook or size needed to obtain gauge
- Tapestry needle
- Beading needle
- Darice Magnetic Canvas: #1195-03 self-adhesive 5 x 8-inch sheet
- 4mm round beads: 2 black
- Face blush
- Spray starch
- Black sewing thread
- Hot-glue gun

GAUGE

4 sc = ½ inch; 4 sc rows = ½ inch

INSTRUCTIONS

BODY

Row 1: With maize, ch 10, sc in 2nd ch from hook and in each ch across, turn. *(9 sc)*

Rows 2–12: Ch 1, sc in each st across, turn.

Row 13: Ch 1, **sc dec** *(see Stitch Guide)* in first 2 sts, sc in each st across to last 2 sts, sc dec in last 2 sts, **do not turn**. Fasten off. *(7 sc)*

Row 14: For **ears**, join white with sc in first st, (hdc, dc, ch 2, dc, hdc, sc) in next st, sl st in each of next 3 sts, (hdc, dc, ch 2, dc, hdc, sc) in next st, sl st in last st, **do not turn**. Fasten off. *(15 sts)*

Row 15: Join maize with sl st in first st, sl st in each of next 2 sts, sl st in next ch, ch 2, sl st in 2nd ch from hook, sl st in next ch, sl st in each of next 3 sts, sc dec in next 3 sts, sl st in each of next 2 sts, sl st in next ch, ch 2, sl st in 2nd ch from hook, sl st in next ch, sl st in each of last 4 sts. Fasten off.

TAIL

With maize, ch 16, hdc in 2nd ch from hook and in each ch across. Fasten off. *(15 hdc)*

TAIL TIP

Row 1: Join white with sl st in last st, 2 sc in end of row, sl st in first ch on opposite side of starting ch, turn. *(2 sc)*

Rows 2 & 3: Ch 1, sc in each sc across, turn.

Row 4: Ch 1, sc dec in next 2 sts. Fasten off.

ASSEMBLY

1. Spray Body and Tail lightly with starch, shape; let dry.

2. With black, sew beads side by side centered to row 12 of Body for eyes.

3. Brush cheeks with blush.

4. With white, using **straight stitch** *(see Fig. 1)*, embroider 3 whiskers to each side of face centered below eyes as shown in photo.

5. With French rose, using straight stitches, embroider small sts for nose at center of whiskers.

6. Glue Tail to bottom of Body, curling up white tip *(see photo)*.

7. Using Kitty as pattern, cut piece magnetic canvas 1/8 inch smaller around outer edge. Attach to back of Kitty. ■

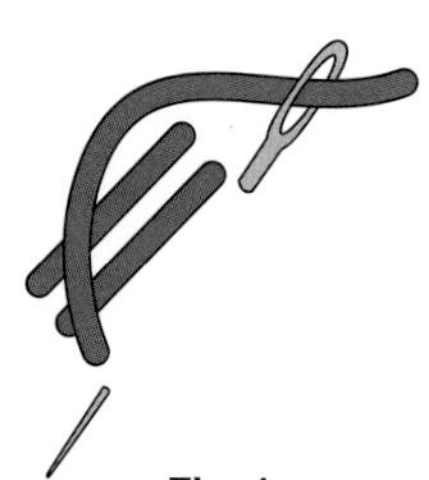

Fig. 1
Straight Stitch

Pig

SKILL LEVEL

EASY

FINISHED SIZE

1 3/8 x 1 1/2 inches

MATERIALS

- Aunt Lydia's Classic Crochet size 10 crochet cotton (350 yds per ball):
  10 yds #401 orchid pink
  2 yds #12 black
- Size 7/1.65mm steel crochet hook or size needed to obtain gauge
- Tapestry needle
- Beading needle
- Darice Magnetic Canvas:
  #1195-03 self-adhesive 5 x 8-inch sheet
- 2 black seed beads
- Face blush
- Spray starch
- Black sewing thread
- Hot-glue gun

GAUGE

5 sc = 1/2 inch; 3 sc rows = 1/2 inch

PATTERN NOTE

Join with slip stitch as indicated unless otherwise stated.

INSTRUCTIONS

FACE

Rnd 1: With orchid pink, ch 2, 8 sc in 2nd ch from hook, **join** *(see Pattern Note)* in beg sc. *(8 sc)*

Rnd 2: Ch 1, 2 sc in each st around, join in beg sc. *(16 sc)*

Rnd 3: Ch 1, 2 sc in first st, sc in next st, [2 sc in next st, sc in next st] around, join in beg sc. *(24 sc)*

Rnd 4: Ch 1, 2 sc in first st, sc in each of next 2 sts, [2 sc in next st, sc in each of next 2 sts] around, join in beg sc. *(32 sc)*

Rnd 5: Ch 1, 2 sc in first st, sc in each of next 3 sts, [2 sc in next st, sc in each of next 3 sts] around, join in beg sc. *(40 sc)*

Row 6: Now working in rows, for **ears**, ch 3, (dc, hdc, sc) in same st, sl st in each of next 5 sts, (sc, hdc, 2 dc) in next st, leaving rem sts unworked. Fasten off.

SNOUT

With orchid pink, ch 4, 10 hdc in 2nd ch from hook, hdc in next ch 10 hdc in last ch, working on opposite side of ch, hdc in next ch, join in top of beg hdc. Fasten off.

ASSEMBLY

1. Spray Body and Snout with starch, shape; let dry.

2. With black, using **straight stitch**, embroider 2 small sts centered on Snout 3/8 inches apart for nostrils *(see photo)*.

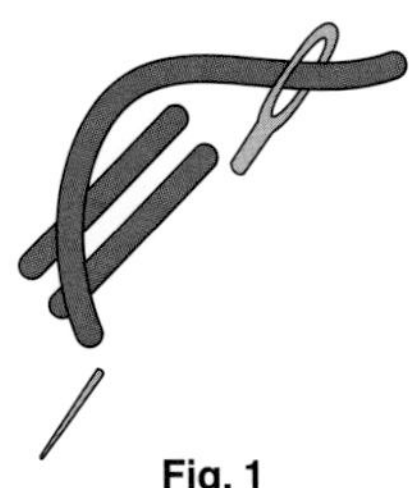

Fig. 1
Straight Stitch

3. Glue Snout centered to Face.

4. With black, sew beads side by side to face centered above Snout.

5. Brush cheeks with blush.

6. Using Pig as pattern, cut piece magnetic canvas 1/8 inch smaller around outer edge. Attach to back of Pig. ■

Signs of the Season

Bunny

SKILL LEVEL

EASY

FINISHED SIZE

1¼ x 2 inches

MATERIALS

- Aunt Lydia's Classic Crochet size 10 crochet cotton (350 yds per ball):
  - 10 yds #420 cream
  - 5 yds #401 orchid pink
- Sizes 10/1.15mm and 7/1.65mm steel crochet hooks or size needed to obtain gauge
- Tapestry needle
- Beading needle
- Darice Magnetic Canvas:
  - #1195-03 self-adhesive 5 x 8-inch sheet
- 4mm round beads: 2 black
- Face blush
- Spray starch
- Black sewing thread
- Hot-glue gun

GAUGE

Size 7 hook: 4 hdc = ½ inch; 3 hdc rows = ½ inch

PATTERN NOTE

Chain-2 at beginning of row counts as first half double crochet unless otherwise stated.

INSTRUCTIONS

BODY

Row 1: With size 7 hook and cream, ch 11, hdc in 2nd ch from hook and in each ch across, turn. *(10 hdc)*

Rows 2–6: **Ch 2** *(see Pattern Note)*, hdc in each st across, turn.

Rows 7–9: Ch 2, **hdc dec** *(see Stitch Guide)* in next 2 sts, hdc in each st across to last 2 sts, hdc dec in last 2 sts, turn. Fasten off at end of last row. *(4 hdc in last row)*

EAR

MAKE 2.

Row 1: With size 10 hook and orchid pink, ch 6, sc in 2nd ch from hook and in each of next 3 chs, (3 sc, ch 1, 3 sc) in last ch, working on opposite side of ch, sc in each of next 4 chs, **do not turn**. Fasten off. *(14 sc)*

Row 2: Working this row in **back lps** *(see Stitch Guide)*, join cream with sc in first st, sc in each st across with (2 sc, ch 1, 2 sc) in ch-1 sp. Fasten off.

NOSE

With size 10 hook and orchid pink, ch 2, 3 sc in 2nd ch from hook. Fasten off.

ASSEMBLY

1. Spray Body, Ears and Nose with starch, shape; let dry.

2. Glue Nose centered to Body over rows 5 and 6. Glue bottom edge of Ears to top edge of Body on WS.

3. With cream, using **straight stitch** *(see Fig. 1)*, embroider long st from bottom edge of Nose to bottom edge of Body.

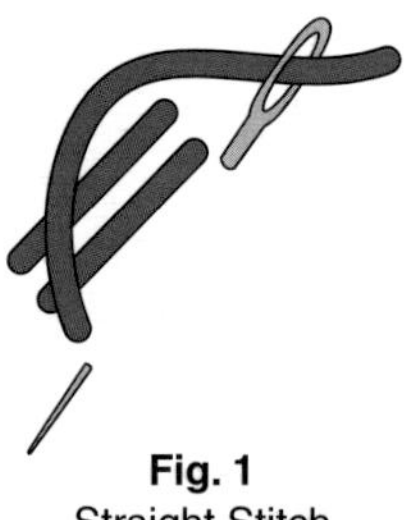

Fig. 1
Straight Stitch

4. Sew beads side by side to Body centered above Nose.

5. Brush cheeks with blush.

6. With cream, using **loop stitch** *(see Fig. 2)*, embroider 3 sts 1 row above eyes *(see photo)*.

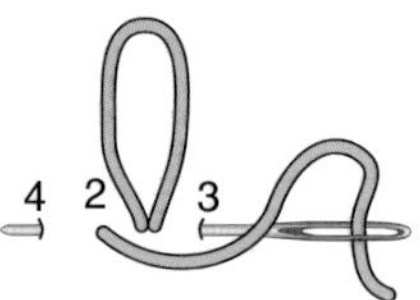

Fig. 2
Loop Stitch

7. Using Bunny as pattern, cut piece magnetic canvas 1/8 inch smaller around outer edge. Attach to back of Bunny. ■

Pumpkin

SKILL LEVEL

EASY

FINISHED SIZE

1⅝ x 2½ inches

MATERIALS

- Aunt Lydia's Classic Crochet size 10 crochet cotton (350 yds per ball):
  15 yds #431 pumpkin
  5 yds each #131 fudge brown and #449 forest green
- Sizes 10/1.15mm and 7/1.65mm steel crochet hooks or size needed to obtain gauge
- Darice Magnetic Canvas: #1195-03 self-adhesive 5 x 8-inch sheet
- 24-gauge floral wire: 4 inches green
- Spray starch
- Hot-glue gun

GAUGE

Size 7 hook: 5 hdc = ½ inch; 3 hdc rows = ½ inch

PATTERN NOTE

Chain-2 at beginning of row counts as first half double crochet unless otherwise stated.

INSTRUCTIONS

PUMPKIN

Row 1: With size 7 hook and pumpkin, ch 13, hdc in 2rd ch from hook and in each ch across, turn. *(12 hdc)*

*Note: Work remaining rows in **back lps** (see Stitch Guide).*

Rows 2 & 3: Ch 2 *(see Pattern Note)*, hdc in same st and in each st across with 2 hdc in last st, turn. *(16 hdc at end of last row)*

Rows 4–7: Ch 2, hdc in each st across, turn.

Row 8: Ch 2, **hdc dec** *(see Stitch Guide)* in next 2 sts, hdc in each st across to last 2 sts, hdc dec in last 2 sts, turn. *(14 hdc)*

Row 9: Ch 2, hdc dec in next 2 sts, hdc in each st across to last 2 sts, hdc dec in last 2 sts. Fasten off. *(12 hdc)*

STEM

Row 1: With size 7 hook and fudge brown, join with sl st in end of row 4, sc in end of row 5, hdc in end of row 6, turn. *(3 sts)*

Row 2: Ch 2, sc in next st, sl st in last st, turn.

Row 3: Ch 1, sl st in first st, sc in next st, hdc in last st, turn.

Row 4: Ch 2, sc in next st, sl st in last st. Fasten off.

LEAF VINE

With size 10 hook and forest green, for **first Leaf**, ch 4, *(sl st, sc, hdc, dc, ch 2, sl st) in each of next 3 chs, sl st in same ch as beg sl st on this leaf*, ch 10, for **2nd Leaf**, rep between * once. Fasten off.

ASSEMBLY

1. Spray Pumpkin and Leaf Vine lightly with starch, shape; let dry.

2. Wrap floral wire around crochet hook to coil. Trim as desired.

3. Glue Leaf Vine and coil to top of Pumpkin as shown in photo.

4. Using Pumpkin as pattern, cut piece magnetic canvas ⅛ inch smaller around outer edge. Attach to back of Pumpkin. ■

Santa

SKILL LEVEL

EASY

FINISHED SIZE

1½ x 2¼ inches

MATERIALS

- Aunt Lydia's Classic Crochet size 10 crochet cotton (white: 400 yds per ball; solids: 350 yds per ball):
  10 yds #1 white
  5 yds each #401 orchid pink, #494 victory red and #420 cream
- Size 7/1.65mm steel crochet hook or size needed to obtain gauge
- Tapestry needle
- Beading needle
- Darice Magnetic Canvas: #1195-03 self-adhesive 5 x 8-inch sheet
- 4mm round beads: 2 black
- 9mm jingle bell: 1 gold
- Face blush
- Spray starch
- Black sewing thread
- Hot-glue gun

GAUGE

4 sc = ½ inch; 4 sc rows = ½ inch

INSTRUCTIONS

FACE

Row 1: With orchid pink, ch 9, sc in 2nd ch from hook and in each ch across, turn. *(8 sc)*

Row 2: Ch 1, sk first st, sc in each st across to last 2 sts, **sc dec** *(see Stitch Guide)* in last 2 sts, turn. *(6 sc)*

Row 3: Ch 1, sc in each st across, turn.

Row 4: Rep row 2. Fasten off. *(4 sc)*

HAT

Row 1: Working in starting ch on opposite side of row 1, join cream with sc in first ch, sc in each ch across, turn. *(8 sc)*

Row 2: Ch 1, sc in each st across, turn.

Row 3: Ch 1, sc in each st across, **do not turn**. Fasten off.

Row 4: Working this row in **back lps** *(see Stitch Guide)*, join victory red with sl st in first st, ch 1, sc dec in first 2 sts, sc in each st across to last 2 sts, sc dec in last 2 sts, turn. *(6 sc)*

Row 5: Ch 1, sc dec in first 2 sts, sc in each st across with 2 sc in last st, turn.

Row 6: Ch 1, 2 sc in first st, sc in each st across to last 2 sts, sc dec in last 2 sts, turn.

Rows 7 & 8: Rep rows 5 and 6.

Row 9: Rep row 5. Fasten off.

BEARD

Row 1: Working in sts and ends of rows around Face, join white with sc in end of row 1 on Hat, evenly sp 14 sc around face to opposite side of row 1 on Hat. Fasten off. *(15 sc)*

Row 2: Join with sl st in first st, sc in same st, *(hdc, 2 dc, hdc) in next st, (sc, sl st) in next st, rep from * across. Fasten off.

MUSTACHE

With white, ch 2, (hdc, 2 dc, hdc, 3 sl sts, hdc, 2 dc, hdc, sl st) in 2nd ch from hook. Fasten off.

Wrap separate strand of white around center of Mustache over 3 sl sts several times, secure.

ASSEMBLY

1. Spray Face and Mustache lightly with starch, shape; let dry.

2. Tack jingle bell to tip of Hat.

3. Sew beads side by side to Face centered below Hat for eyes.

4. Brush cheeks with blush.

5. Glue Mustache to Face centered below eyes.

6. Using Santa as pattern, cut piece magnetic canvas ⅛ inch smaller around outer edge. Attach to back of Santa. ■

Shamrock

SKILL LEVEL

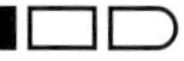
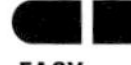

EASY

FINISHED SIZE
2 x 2⅛ inches

MATERIALS

- Aunt Lydia's Classic Crochet size 10 crochet cotton (350 yds per ball):
  15 yds #484 myrtle green
- Size 10/1.15mm steel crochet hook or size needed to obtain gauge
- Darice Magnetic Canvas:
  #1195-03 self-adhesive 5 x 8-inch sheet
- Spray starch

GAUGE
5 sc = ½ inch; 5 sc rows = ½ inch

PATTERN NOTES
Join with slip stitch as indicated unless otherwise stated.

Chain-3 at beginning of row counts as first double crochet unless otherwise stated.

INSTRUCTIONS
SHAMROCK
Rnd 1: Ch 2, 6 sc in 2nd ch from hook, **join** *(see Pattern Notes)* in beg sc. *(6 sc)*

Rnd 2: Ch 1, 2 sc in each st around, join in beg sc. *(12 sc)*

FIRST LEAF
Row 1: Ch 1, 2 sc in first st, sc in next st, 2 sc in next st, leaving rem sts unworked, turn. *(5 sc)*

Rows 2–4: Ch 1, 2 sc in first st, sc in each st across with 2 sc in last st, turn. *(11 sc at end of last row)*

Row 5: Ch 3 *(see Pattern Notes)*, dc in same st, hdc in next st, sc in each of next 7 sts, hdc in next st, 2 dc in last st, turn. *(13 sts)*

Row 6: Ch 3, dc in next st, hdc in each of next 2 sts, sc in each of next 5 sts, hdc in each of next 2 sts, dc in next st, hdc in last st, turn.

Row 7: Ch 2 *(counts as first hdc)*, dc in next st, hdc in each of next 3 sts, sl st in each of next 3 sts, hdc in each of next 3 sts, dc in next st, (hdc, sl st) in last st. Fasten off.

NEXT LEAF
Row 1: Join with sc in next unworked st on rnd 2 of Shamrock, sc in same st, sc in next st, 2 sc in next st, leaving rem sts unworked, turn. *(5 sc)*

Rows 2–7: Rep rows 2–7 of First Leaf.

Rep Next Leaf 1 more time.

STEM

Row 1: Join with sc in next unworked st on rnd 2 of Shamrock, hdc in next st, dc in last st, turn. *(3 sts)*

Row 2: Ch 3, hdc in next st, sc in last st, turn.

Row 3: Ch 1, sc in first st, hdc in next st, dc in last st, turn.

Rows 4 & 5: Rep rows 2 and 3.

Row 6: Rep row 2. Fasten off.

ASSEMBLY

1. Spray Shamrock with starch, shape; let dry.

2. Using Shamrock as pattern, cut piece magnetic canvas 1/8 inch smaller around outer edge. Attach to back of Shamrock. ■

Turkey

SKILL LEVEL

EASY

FINISHED SIZE

2 3/4 x 3 1/4 inches

MATERIALS

- Aunt Lydia's Classic Crochet size 10 crochet cotton (350 yds per ball):
  10 yds each #494 victory red, #421 goldenrod, #449 forest green, #431 pumpkin
  5 yds #310 copper mist
- Sizes 10/1.15mm and 7/1.65mm steel crochet hooks or size needed to obtain gauge
- Beading needle
- Darice Magnetic Canvas: #1195-03 self-adhesive 5 x 8-inch sheet
- 4mm round beads: 2 black
- Spray starch
- Black sewing thread
- Hot-glue gun

GAUGE

Size 7 hook: 5 hdc = 1/2 inch; 3 hdc rows = 1/2 inch

PATTERN NOTE

Chain-2 at beginning of row counts as first half double crochet unless otherwise stated.

SPECIAL STITCH

Picot: Ch 3, sl st in 3rd ch from hook.

INSTRUCTIONS

BODY

Row 1: With size 7 hook and copper mist, ch 6, hdc in 2nd ch from hook and in each ch across, turn. *(5 hdc)*

Rows 2 & 3: **Ch 2** *(see Pattern Note)*, hdc in same st, hdc in each st across with 2 hdc in last st, turn. *(9 hdc at end of last row)*

Rows 4 & 5: Ch 2, hdc in each st across, turn.

Rows 6 & 7: Ch 2, **hdc dec** *(see Stitch Guide)* in next 2 sts, hdc in each st across to last 2 sts, hdc dec in last 2 sts, turn. *(5 hdc at end of last row)*

Row 8: Ch 2, hdc in each of next 2 sts, hdc dec in last 2 sts, turn. *(4 hdc)*

Rows 9–11: Ch 2, hdc in each st across, turn. Fasten off at end of last row.

BEAK
With size 10 hook and goldenrod, ch 2, 2 sc in 2nd ch from hook. Fasten off.

WATTLE
With size 10 hook and victory red, ch 6, 3 sl st in 2nd ch from hook, sl st in each of next 4 chs. Fasten off.

TAIL

Row 1: With size 10 hook and victory red, ch 14, sl st in 2nd ch from hook and in each of next 2 chs, sc in each of next 5 chs, hdc in each of next 5 chs, **picot** *(see Special Stitch)*, turn. *(13 sts, 1 picot)*

Row 2: Ch 1, hdc in each of first 5 sts, sc in each of next 5 sts, sl st in each of last 3 sts, turn. Fasten off.

Row 3: Working this row in **back lps** *(see Stitch Guide)*, join goldenrod with sl st in first st, sl st in each of next 2 sts, sc in each of next 5 sts, hdc in each of last 5 sts, picot, turn.

Row 4: Ch 1, hdc in each of first 5 sts, sc in each of next 5 sts, sl st in each of last 3 sts, turn. Fasten off.

Rows 5–34: Working in color sequence of forest green, pumpkin, victory red and goldenrod, [rep rows 3 and 4 alternately] 15 times.

ASSEMBLY

1. Spray Body, Beak, Wattle and Tail lightly with starch, shape; let dry.

2. Sew beads side by side to row 10 of Body for eyes.

3. Glue Wattle centered below eyes with narrow end at top.

4. Glue Beak centered below eyes over top edge of Wattle.

5. Glue Body centered to top of Tail as shown in photo.

6. Using Turkey as pattern, cut piece magnetic canvas ⅛ inch smaller around outer edge. Attach to back of Turkey. ■

Tropical Treasures

Flamingo

SKILL LEVEL

EASY

FINISHED SIZE
2½ x 3½ inches

MATERIALS

- Aunt Lydia's Classic Crochet size 10 crochet cotton (350 yds per ball):
  - 10 yds #332 hot pink
  - 5 yds each #493 French rose and #12 black

- Size 7/1.65mm steel crochet hook or size needed to obtain gauge
- Beading needle
- Darice Magnetic Canvas: #1195-03 self-adhesive 5 x 8-inch sheet
- 4mm round bead: 1 black
- Spray starch
- Black sewing thread
- Hot-glue gun

GAUGE

4 sc = ½ inch; 5 sc rows = ½ inch

INSTRUCTIONS

BODY

Row 1: With hot pink, ch 6, sc in 2nd ch from hook and in each ch across, turn. *(5 sc)*

Rows 2–5: Ch 1, 2 sc in first st, sc in each st across with 2 sc in last st, turn. *(13 sc at end of last row)*

Row 6: Ch 1, 2 sc in first st, sc in each st across, turn. *(14 sc)*

Rows 7 & 8: Rep row 2. *(18 sts at end of last row)*

Row 9: Ch 1, sc in each st across with 2 sc in last st, turn. Fasten off. *(19 sc)*

LEGS

Row 1: Sk first 7 sts of row 9 on Body, join hot pink with sc in next st, sc in each of next 2 sts, leaving rem sts unworked, **do not turn**. Fasten off. *(3 sc)*

Row 2: Join French rose with sl st in first st, for **first Leg**, *ch 16, sl st in 2nd ch from hook, 3 sl st in next ch, ch 1, sl st in each of last 13 chs*, sl st in next st on last row, for **2nd Leg**, rep between * once, sl st in last st on last row. Fasten off.

NECK

Join hot pink in end of row 8 on left-hand side of Body, ch 21, for **head**, 8 hdc in 2nd ch from hook, sc in each of next 17 chs, hdc in next ch, 2 hdc in last ch, sl st in next st on row 9 of Body. Fasten off.

BEAK

Row 1: Join hot pink with sl st in 5th hdc on head, **ch 2** *(counts as first hdc)*, hdc in same st, hdc in next st, **do not turn**. Fasten off.

Row 2: Join black with sl st in first st, ch 4, sl st in 2nd ch from hook and in each of next 2 chs, sl st in last st on last row. Fasten off.

ASSEMBLY

1. Spray Flamingo lightly with starch, shape, tacking end of Beak to Neck, and back of Neck to Body as shown in photo; let dry.

2. Sew bead to head for eye.

3. Cross left-hand Leg over right-hand Leg and tack to secure.

4. Using Body as pattern, cut piece magnetic canvas ⅛ inch smaller around outer edge. Attach to back of Body. Rep using head as pattern. ■

Flip-Flop

SKILL LEVEL

EASY

FINISHED SIZE

1¼ x 2¼ inches

MATERIALS

- Aunt Lydia's Classic Crochet size 10 crochet cotton (solids: 350 yds per ball; multis: 300 yds per ball):
  10 yds #250 Mexicana
  5 yds #12 black
- Size 7/1.65mm steel crochet hook or size needed to obtain gauge
- Darice Magnetic Canvas:
  #1195-03 self-adhesive 5 x 8-inch sheet
- Spray starch

GAUGE

4 sc = ½ inch; 5 sc rows = ½ inch

INSTRUCTIONS

FLIP-FLOP

Row 1: With Mexicana, ch 7, sc in 2nd ch from hook and in each ch across, turn. *(6 sc)*

Rows 2 & 3: Ch 1, 2 sc in first st, sc in each st across with 2 sc in last st, turn. *(10 sc at end of last row)*

Rows 4–7: Ch 1, sc in each st across, turn.

Row 8: Ch 1, **sc dec** *(see Stitch Guide)* in first 2 sts, sc in each st across to last 2 sts, sc dec in last 2 sts, turn. *(8 sc)*

Rows 9–16: Ch 1, sc in each st across, turn.

Rows 17–18: Ch 1, sc dec in first 2 sts, sc in each st across to last 2 sts, sc dec in last 2 sts, turn. Fasten off at end of last row. *(4 sc at end of last row)*

EDGING AND STRAP

Join black with sc in end of row 9, evenly sp sts, sc in ends of rows and sts around outer edge, join with sl st in beg sc, ch 7, sc around st at center of row 2, ch 7, sl st in st at opposite end of row 9. Fasten off.

ASSEMBLY

1. Spray Flip-Flop lightly with starch, shape; let dry.

2. Using Flip-Flop as pattern, cut piece magnetic canvas ⅛ inch smaller around outer edge. Attach to back of Flip-Flop. ■

Palm Tree

SKILL LEVEL

EASY

FINISHED SIZE

2⅜ x 3¾ inches

MATERIALS

- Aunt Lydia's Classic Crochet size 10 crochet cotton (350 yds per ball):
  15 yds each #310 copper mist and #484 myrtle green
- Size 7/1.65mm steel crochet hook or size needed to obtain gauge
- Darice Magnetic Canvas:
  #1195-03 self-adhesive 5 x 8-inch sheet
- Spray starch

GAUGE

4 sts = ½ inch, 4 sc rows = ½ inch

PATTERN NOTE

Chain-2 at beginning of row counts as first half double crochet unless otherwise stated.

INSTRUCTIONS

TREE

Row 1: With copper mist, ch 7, sl st in 2nd ch from hook, sl st in next ch, sc in each of next 2 chs, hdc in each of last 2 chs, turn. *(6 sts)*

Row 2: Ch 2 *(see Pattern Note)*, hdc in next st, sc in each of next 2 sts, sl st in each of last 2 sts, turn.

Row 3: Working this row in **back lps** *(see Stitch Guide)*, ch 2, hdc in next st, sc in each of next 2 sts, sl st in each of last 2 sts, turn.

Row 4: Ch 1, sl st in each of first 2 sts, sc in each of next 2 sts, hdc in each of last 2 sts, turn.

Row 5: Working this row in back lps, ch 1, sl st in each of first 2 sts, sc in each of next 2 sts, hdc in each of last 2 sts, turn.

Row 6: Ch 2, hdc in next st, sc in each of next 2 sts, sl st in each of last 2 sts, turn.

Rows 7–18: [Rep rows 3–6 consecutively] 3 times.

Rows 19–21: Rep rows 3–5. Fasten off at end of last row.

Row 22: Join myrtle green with sl st in first st, ch 11, sl st in 2nd ch from hook, sl st in next ch, sc in each of next 2 chs, 2 hdc in each of next 2 chs, 2 dc in each of last 4 chs, dc in next st as beg sl st, dc in each of last 5 sts, turn. *(22 sts)*

Row 23: Ch 11, sl st in 2nd ch from hook, sl st in next ch, sc in each of next 2 chs, 2 hdc in each of next 2 chs, 2 dc in each of last 4 chs, sc in each of next 6 sts, leaving rem sts unworked, turn.

Row 24: Ch 9, sl st in 2nd ch from hook, sl st in next ch, sc in each of next 2 chs, 2 hdc in each of next 2 chs, dc in each of next 2 chs, sc in each of next 6 sts, leaving rem sts unworked, turn. *(16 sts)*

Row 25: Rep row 24.

Row 26: Ch 8, sl st in 2nd ch from hook, sl st in next ch, sc in each of next 2 chs, 2 hdc in each of next 2 chs, 2 dc in last ch, sc in each of next 6 sts, leaving rem sts unworked, turn. *(16 sts)*

Row 27: Ch 8, sl st in 2nd ch from hook, sl st in next ch, sc in each of next 2 chs, 2 hdc in each of next 2 chs, 2 dc in last ch, sc in each of next 2 sts, leaving rem sts unworked, **do not turn.** *(12 sts)*

Row 28: Ch 8, sl st in 2nd ch from hook, sl st in next ch, sc in each of next 2 chs, 2 hdc in each of next 2 chs, 2 dc in last ch, sk next st, sl st in next st. Fasten off.

ASSEMBLY

1. Spray Tree lightly with starch, shape; let dry.

2. Using Tree as pattern, cut piece magnetic canvas 1/8 inch smaller around outer edge. Attach to back of Tree. ■

Sunglasses

SKILL LEVEL

EASY

FINISHED SIZE

3/4 x 2 inches

MATERIALS

- Aunt Lydia's Classic Crochet size 10 crochet cotton (350 yds per ball):
  5 yds each #451 parakeet and #12 black
- Size 7/1.65mm steel crochet hook or size needed to obtain gauge
- Darice Magnetic Canvas:
  #1195-03 self-adhesive 5 x 8-inch sheet
- Spray starch

GAUGE

4 sc = 1/2 inch, 4 sc rows = 1/2 inch

INSTRUCTIONS

SUNGLASSES

TOP FRAME

Row 1: With parakeet, ch 16, sc in 2nd ch from hook and in each ch across, turn. *(15 sc)*

Row 2: Ch 1, sc in each st across, **do not turn.** Fasten off.

FIRST LENS

Row 1: Working this row in **back lps** *(see Stitch Guide)*, join black with sc in 2nd st of last row, sc in each of next 5 sts, leaving rem sts unworked, turn. *(6 sc)*

Row 2: Ch 1, **sc dec** *(see Stitch Guide)* in first 2 sts, sc in each of next 2 sts, sc dec in last 2 sts, turn. *(4 sc)*

Row 3: Ch 1, sc dec in first 2 sts, sc dec in last 2 sts. Fasten off.

2ND LENS

Row 1: Working this row in back lps, sk next unworked st on last row of Top Frame, join black with sc in next st, sc in each of next 5 sts, leaving last st unworked, turn. *(6 sc)*

Rows 2 & 3: Rep rows 2 and 3 of First Lens.

BOTTOM FRAME

Join parakeet with sc in first skipped st of row 2 on Top Frame, *evenly sp 4 sc across ends of rows on First Lens, 2 sc in back lps of each of next 2 sts, evenly sp 4 sc across ends of rows*, sc in next unworked st on row 2 at center of Top Frame, working on 2nd Lens, rep between * once, sc in last unworked st on row 2 of Top Frame. Fasten off.

ASSEMBLY

1. Spray Sunglasses lightly with starch, shape; let dry.

2. Using Sunglasses as pattern, cut piece magnetic canvas 1/8 inch smaller around outer edge. Attach to back of Sunglasses. ■

T-Shirt

SKILL LEVEL

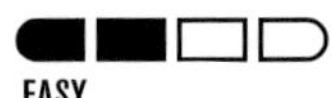

EASY

FINISHED SIZE

1⅞ x 2½ inches

MATERIALS

- Aunt Lydia's Classic Crochet size 10 crochet cotton (350 yds per ball):
  20 yds #431 pumpkin
- Size 7/1.65mm steel crochet hook or size needed to obtain gauge
- Darice Magnetic Canvas:
  #1195-03 self-adhesive 5 x 8-inch sheet
- Spray starch

GAUGE

4 sc = ½ inch, 4 sc rows = ½ inch

INSTRUCTIONS

T-SHIRT

BODY

Row 1: Ch 13, sc in 2nd ch from hook and in each ch across, turn. *(12 sc)*

Rows 2–11: Ch 1, sc in each st across, turn.

FIRST SHOULDER

Row 1: Ch 1, sc in each of first 3 sts, **sc dec** *(see Stitch Guide)* in next 2 sts, leaving rem sts unworked, turn. *(4 sc)*

Row 2: Ch 1, sc dec in first 2 sts, sc in each of last 2 sts, turn. *(3 sc)*

Rows 3–5: Ch 1, sc in each st across, turn. Fasten off at end of last row.

2ND SHOULDER

Row 1: Sk next 2 sts on last row of Body, join with sl st in next st, ch 1, sc dec in same st and next st, sc in each of last 3 sts, turn. *(4 sc)*

Row 2: Ch 1, sc in each of first 2 sts, sc dec in last 2 sts, turn. *(3 sc)*

Rows 3–5: Ch 1, sc in each st across, turn. Fasten off at end of last row.

FIRST SLEEVE

Row 1: Join with sc in end of row 11 on right-hand side of Body, sc in each of next 5 rows, turn. *(6 sc)*

Rows 2–5: Ch 1, sc in each st across, turn. Fasten off at end of last row.

2ND SLEEVE

Row 1: Join with sc in end of row 5 on left-hand shoulder, sc in end of each of next 5 rows, turn. *(6 sc)*

Rows 2–5: Ch 1, sc in each st across, turn. Fasten off at end of last row.

ASSEMBLY

1. Spray T-Shirt lightly with starch, shape; let dry.

2. Using T-Shirt as pattern, cut piece magnetic canvas ⅛ inch smaller around outer edge. Attach to back of T-Shirt. ■

Stitch Guide

For more complete information, visit **FreePatterns.com**

ABBREVIATIONS

beg	begin/begins/beginning
bpdc	back post double crochet
bpsc	back post single crochet
bptr	back post treble crochet
CC	contrasting color
ch(s)	chain(s)
ch-	refers to chain or space previously made (e.g., ch-1 space)
ch sp(s)	chain space(s)
cl(s)	cluster(s)
cm	centimeter(s)
dc	double crochet (singular/plural)
dc dec	double crochet 2 or more stitches together, as indicated
dec	decrease/decreases/decreasing
dtr	double treble crochet
ext	extended
fpdc	front post double crochet
fpsc	front post single crochet
fptr	front post treble crochet
g	gram(s)
hdc	half double crochet
hdc dec	half double crochet 2 or more stitches together, as indicated
inc	increase/increases/increasing
lp(s)	loop(s)
MC	main color
mm	millimeter(s)
oz	ounce(s)
pc	popcorn(s)
rem	remain/remains/remaining
rep(s)	repeat(s)
rnd(s)	round(s)
RS	right side
sc	single crochet (singular/plural)
sc dec	single crochet 2 or more stitches together, as indicated
sk	skip/skipped/skipping
sl st(s)	slip stitch(es)
sp(s)	space/spaces/spaced
st(s)	stitch(es)
tog	together
tr	treble crochet
trtr	triple treble
WS	wrong side
yd(s)	yard(s)
yo	yarn over

Chain—ch: Yo, pull through lp on hook.

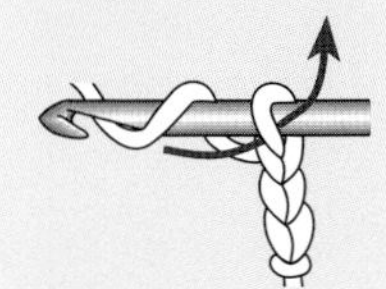

Slip stitch—sl st: Insert hook in st, pull through both lps on hook.

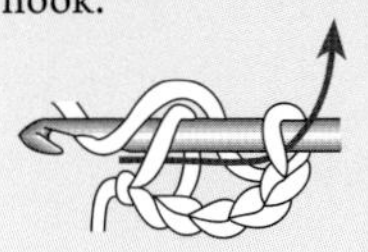

Single crochet—sc: Insert hook in st, yo, pull through st, yo, pull through both lps on hook.

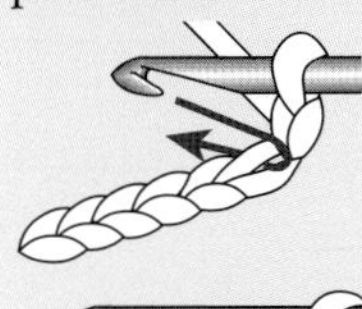

Front post stitch—fp:
Back post stitch—bp: When working post st, insert hook from right to left around post st on previous row.

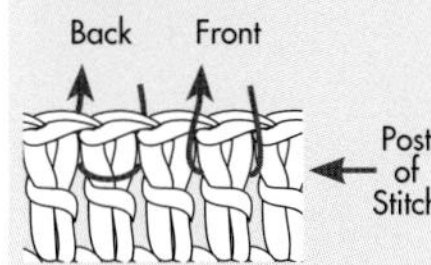

Front loop—front lp
Back loop—back lp

Half double crochet—hdc: Yo, insert hook in st, yo, pull through st, yo, pull through all 3 lps on hook.

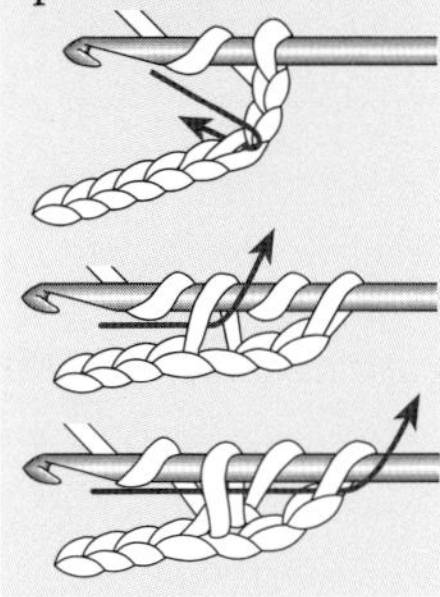

Double crochet—dc: Yo, insert hook in st, yo, pull through st, [yo, pull through 2 lps] twice.

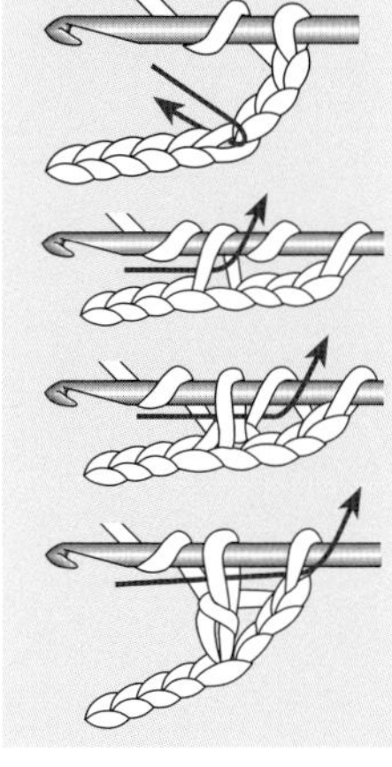

Change colors: Drop first color; with 2nd color, pull through last 2 lps of st.

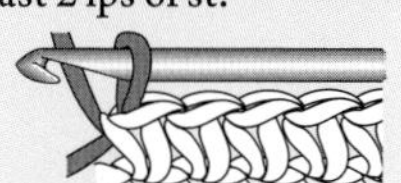

Treble crochet—tr: Yo twice, insert hook in st, yo, pull through st, [yo, pull through 2 lps] 3 times.

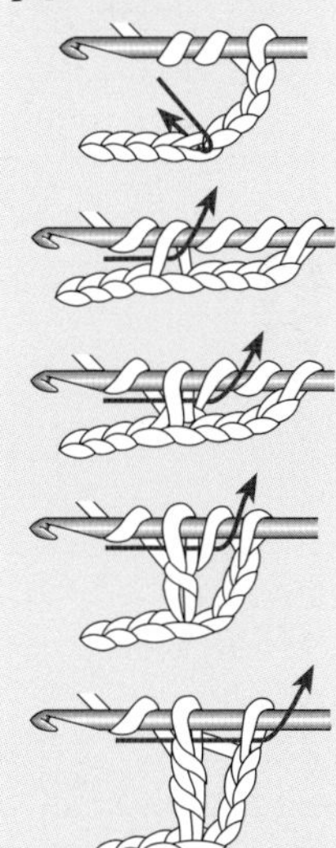

Double treble crochet—dtr: Yo 3 times, insert hook in st, yo, pull through st, [yo, pull through 2 lps] 4 times.

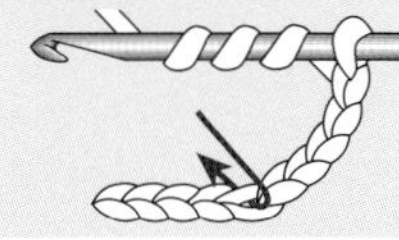

Single crochet decrease (sc dec): (Insert hook, yo, draw lp through) in each of the sts indicated, yo, draw through all lps on hook.

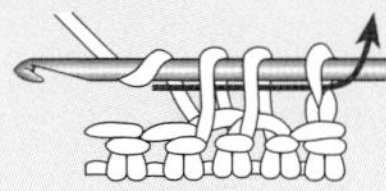

Example of 2-sc dec

Half double crochet decrease (hdc dec): (Yo, insert hook, yo, draw lp through) in each of the sts indicated, yo, draw through all lps on hook.

Example of 2-hdc dec

Double crochet decrease (dc dec): (Yo, insert hook, yo, draw loop through, draw through 2 lps on hook) in each of the sts indicated, yo, draw through all lps on hook.

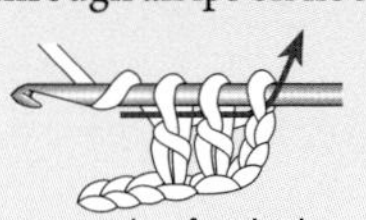

Example of 2-dc dec

Example of 2-tr dec

Treble crochet decrease (tr dec): Holding back last lp of each st, tr in each of the sts indicated, yo, pull through all lps on hook.

US		**UK**
sl st (slip stitch)	=	sc (single crochet)
sc (single crochet)	=	dc (double crochet)
hdc (half double crochet)	=	htr (half treble crochet)
dc (double crochet)	=	tr (treble crochet)
tr (treble crochet)	=	dtr (double treble crochet)
dtr (double treble crochet)	=	ttr (triple treble crochet)
skip	=	miss

Metric Conversion Charts

METRIC CONVERSIONS				
yards	x	.9144	=	metres (m)
yards	x	91.44	=	centimetres (cm)
inches	x	2.54	=	centimetres (cm)
inches	x	25.40	=	millimetres (mm)
inches	x	.0254	=	metres (m)

centimetres	x	.3937	=	inches
metres	x	1.0936	=	yards

INCHES INTO MILLIMETRES & CENTIMETRES (Rounded off slightly)

inches	mm	cm	inches	cm	inches	cm	inches	cm
1/8	3	0.3	5	12.5	21	53.5	38	96.5
1/4	6	0.6	5 1/2	14	22	56	39	99
3/8	10	1	6	15	23	58.5	40	101.5
1/2	13	1.3	7	18	24	61	41	104
5/8	15	1.5	8	20.5	25	63.5	42	106.5
3/4	20	2	9	23	26	66	43	109
7/8	22	2.2	10	25.5	27	68.5	44	112
1	25	2.5	11	28	28	71	45	114.5
1 1/4	32	3.2	12	30.5	29	73.5	46	117
1 1/2	38	3.8	13	33	30	76	47	119.5
1 3/4	45	4.5	14	35.5	31	79	48	122
2	50	5	15	38	32	81.5	49	124.5
2 1/2	65	6.5	16	40.5	33	84	50	127
3	75	7.5	17	43	34	86.5		
3 1/2	90	9	18	46	35	89		
4	100	10	19	48.5	36	91.5		
4 1/2	115	11.5	20	51	37	94		

KNITTING NEEDLES CONVERSION CHART

Canada/U.S.	0	1	2	3	4	5	6	7	8	9	10	10½	11	13	15
Metric (mm)	2	2¼	2¾	3¼	3½	3¾	4	4½	5	5½	6	6½	8	9	10

CROCHET HOOKS CONVERSION CHART

Canada/U.S.	1/B	2/C	3/D	4/E	5/F	6/G	8/H	9/I	10/J	10½/K	N
Metric (mm)	2.25	2.75	3.25	3.5	3.75	4.25	5	5.5	6	6.5	9.0

TOLL-FREE ORDER LINE or to request a free catalog (800) LV-ANNIE (800) 582-6643
Customer Service (800) AT-ANNIE (800) 282-6643, **Fax** (800) 882-6643
Visit AnniesAttic.com

ISBN: 978-1-59635-284-1

Printed in USA

1 2 3 4 5 6 7 8 9